MENLO SCHOOL · MENLO COLLEGE

founded 1915

WHO WAS?

General Editor of the Series: Jean Leymarie

WHO WAS

RAPHAEL?

Distributed in the United States by
THE WORLD PUBLISHING COMPANY
2231 West 110th Street, Cleveland 2, Ohio

★

© 1967, by Editions d'Art Albert Skira, Geneva
Library of Congress Catalog Card Number: 67-25119

TEXT BY NELLO PONENTE

TRANSLATED FROM THE ITALIAN BY JAMES EMMONS

CONTENTS

RAPHAEL is probably the best known and best loved of all painters. The pictures he painted nearly five centuries ago have entered into the store of our visual memories, into our very lives. They belong to the common stock of images which we take for granted, without realizing how much poorer we should be without them. For almost five centuries his radiant and noble forms have represented one of the highest ideals of our civilization. In the popular mind the name Raphael is synonymous with painting. Even today, when so many links with the past have been weakened or severed, a Madonna has for us the face that Raphael gave her, a philosopher the beard of Aristotle in the *School of Athens*, a pope the ostentation of Leo X. These forms, this embodied dignity, grace, and wisdom, still correspond to an ideal, even though we admit it to be unattainable. They stand as a token and symbol of all that the human spirit aspires to, and a solace to it in times of failure. But familiarity with them has diverted attention from the historical and aesthetic values they represent. In our contemporary culture, with its insatiable appetite for images, the forms of beauty created by Raphael have been used and abused, reproduced again and again, put to other purposes without regard to these values, precisely because of their recognized appeal, their undiminished potency as image and illustration, though no longer as a source of emotion and knowledge.

The artists of the nineteenth and twentieth centuries have pursued other ideals. They have turned away from the conventionalized beauty associated with Raphael and created a very different conception of beauty, dictated by other necessities, conditioned by their own time, by a different relation to history. Cézanne could propose to "do Poussin over again from nature," but from what nature could he have done Raphael over again? The *Montagne Sainte-Victoire* has nothing in common with the *Parnassus*, nor Emile Zola with Baldassare Castiglione. Renoir discovered the "wisdom" of Raphael by looking at him through the eyes of Ingres: he was thrown off his balance and only regained it when he had worked Raphael out of his system. The Pre-Raphaelites, in their cult of the Middle Ages, charged Raphael with having introduced into painting a "norm" which clipped the wings of spontaneity. Even Baudelaire pronounced judgment against him. But not his friend Delacroix. This is worth emphasizing, for it shows how much the values Raphael stands for could still mean to a great modern artist. On January 25, 1857, Delacroix made this entry in his diary: "The first features in which a skillful master outlines his thought contain in embryo everything remarkable in the finished work. When Raphael, Rembrandt, Poussin —these I name on purpose because they stand out as men of thought—draw a few lines on paper, not a single one seems irrelevant. For intelligent eyes, those lines spring to life at once, and nothing in the development of the theme, apparently so vague, will diverge from this initial conception, barely unfolding yet already complete.''

Intelligent eyes will perceive in Raphael the ''thought,'' the ''wisdom,'' even the ''norm,'' but they will go on to perceive the values these represent, and to appreciate their full importance in the artistic and spiritual growth of modern man. There is, then, good reason to concern ourselves with Raphael and to offer here, to the intelligent eyes of the reader, a considered view of an artist who ranks among the outstanding spokesmen of the civilization of the Renaissance, an artist whom we hold to be not merely one of the glories of the past but a living force. May the following pages help to bring home a message which, in the simplicity of its immediate appeal and the range of its implications and associations, is communicable on many levels, and still relevant on them all.

Chapter One

Urbino,
Light of Italy

View of Urbino with the Ducal Palace.

RAPHAEL was born at Urbino on the 6th of April 1483, the son of Giovanni Santi, a painter, and his wife Magia di Battista Ciarla. Seven months had passed since the death of Federico di Montefeltro, Duke of Urbino, which was later described by Baldassare Castiglione as the "light of Italy." To be born in Urbino at that time was something of a privilege: this little hill town in central Italy had become an outstanding cultural center, open to all the new ideas and speculations of the Renaissance. Duke Federico had personified the ideal of the scholar prince, the accomplished humanist who knows how necessary culture is for the proper exercise of political power. A skilled and successful military leader, and a shrewd politician, he had extended the territory of his duchy from Urbino to Gubbio, from the Marches to Umbria, and embellished it with works of art. He loved books, and the great library he built up in his palace at Urbino was admired and praised by the humanists. "He spared neither cost nor pains," wrote his librarian Vespasiano da Bisticci, "and when he heard of any fine book, whether in Italy or outside Italy, he would

Courtyard of the Ducal Palace of Urbino, designed after 1468 by Luciano Laurana (1420-1479).

send for it. It is now fourteen years or more since he began to collect this library, and he has always employed, in Urbino, in Florence and in other places, thirty or forty scribes in his service." No wonder that Cristoforo Landino dedicated to Federico his *Camaldulensian Disputations*, a series of imaginary conversations between Leon Battista Alberti and Lorenzo de' Medici, written about 1475. This book is a landmark in the development of the Neo-Platonic philosophy of the humanists.

Urbino, then, was not merely the small, outlying seat of a local duchy, a prey to the political struggles of this stormy period (Urbino was treacherously captured and occupied by Cesare Borgia in 1502-1503). It was one of the most civilized places in Europe, a place where for three generations, under the Montefeltro, then under the Della Rovere family, the reigning Duke tried to live up to the moral and cultural ideals of the Italian Renaissance. Impressed by the virtues he saw put into practice at Urbino, where he came to live under Duke Guidobaldo whom he served as special envoy and ambassador, Baldassare Castiglione wrote *The Book of the Courtier:* one of the most significant documents of the period and one of the finest works of Italian literature. It defines not so much a code of good manners as a complete standard of behavior for the perfect gentleman, the man of honor and decency "who is more than proficient in letters, at least in those studies which we call the humanities, and is acquainted not only with Latin, but with Greek as well, on account of the many and various things which in that tongue are sublimely written. Let him be versed in the poets and no less in the orators and historians, and skilled too in the writing of verse and prose, more especially in this our own tongue."

Raphael was born and bred in these cultivated, idealistic circles where, however, life was never at a standstill—on the contrary. At the court of Urbino, speculation and self-expression were encouraged and men lived in full consciousness of the splendid achievements of Italian art in the second half of the fifteenth century. It was in Rome that Raphael rose to his greatest glory, patronized by a very different court, that of the popes Julius II and Leo X, of which he made himself an incomparable interpreter. But the ideals of Urbino stayed with him always, going far to shape both his art and his view of life. For at Urbino he had become aware of the new position the artist had won for himself in society; he had seen the high status accorded to the artist's work in recognition of its power to shed glory on a prince at least as much as any political activity. It is significant that Duke Federico himself, in the letter of 1468 in which he commissioned Luciano Laurana to design the ducal palace, gave the architect a free hand to perform "whatever we ourself might do if we were present." In the anonymous painting in the Naples museum, it is probably Federico's son Guidobaldo who is portrayed almost as a disciple beside Luca Pacioli, the mathematician who disseminated the principles of perspective laid down by Piero della Francesca.

Among the artists who worked at Urbino before Raphael's time were Piero della Francesca and Melozzo da Forlì; the Flemish master Justus of Ghent, who together with the Spaniard Pedro Berruguete decorated Federico's study with portraits of twenty-eight famous men; the architect Luciano Laurana; the engineer and architect Francesco di Giorgio Martini, who designed the ducal palace at Gubbio and was also a painter, sculptor and writer of treatises. All were men of the Renaissance, not only in the confident rationalism of their outlook but in their lofty sense of purpose and their cult of knowledge, universal knowledge, for its own sake. They were conscious of having overleaped the limitations and restraints which the medieval artist had accepted in all humility. They had, in a word, achieved a higher status for the artist. Art, now, was a liberal profession. More, the artist was a creator, an inventor of forms governed by well-defined laws of proportion, forms which in themselves gave rise to an exemplary style, not through the random play of impulse and imagination but through reason, the thinking mind, a rational view of the world. Artists, then, were no longer merely artisans, masters of a craft, but men with a truth and a vision to propound. This new pride and purposefulness were shared by the humanist writers and scholars. Over a century before this, a man of letters, Boccaccio, had praised Giotto for

Piero della Francesca (about 1420-1492). Allegory of the ▶ Triumph of Federico di Montefeltro.

This scene is painted on one of the two panels of a diptych. On the other side of them are portraits of Federico di Montefeltro and his wife Battista Sforza. Painted after 1472. Uffizi, Florence.

Portrait of Luca Pacioli with One of his Pupils. Museo di Capodimonte, Naples.

The Franciscan friar Luca Pacioli was the most famous mathematician of his day and a prolific writer on mathematical subjects. During the second half of the fifteenth century he taught in different cities in Italy. In the 1490's he was at the court of Ludovico il Moro in Milan, where he met Bramante and Leonardo. He was also friendly with Leon Battista Alberti and Piero della Francesca. To the latter he owed the theory of proportions which he expounded in his "Treatise on the Divine Proportion," published in Venice in 1509 with drawings by Leonardo. This picture is signed "Jaco. Bar. Vigennis" and dated 1495, but the artist has never been identified.

"restoring to the light that art which, for many centuries, through the mistaken ways of those who painted rather to charm the eyes of the ignorant than to gratify the intelligence of the wise, had lain in its grave." The closed world of medieval scholasticism broke down and fell apart with the revival of independent thought fostered by the study of Plato (whose dialogues were the model and inspiration of Landino's *Disputations*): the same emancipation was taking place in art.

It is true that Raphael, as Vasari pointed out as early as the sixteenth century, had neither the intellectual insight of Leonardo nor the visionary power and revolutionary drive of Michelangelo. But it was Raphael who better than any other artist expressed the mood and ideals of his contemporaries; he became the most popular and best loved artist of the time because his art, in its happy marriage of contrasts, reconciles better than any other the antagonisms and cross purposes of this complex period. For this very reason, for the serene mastery with which he smoothes over those antagonisms, the fact of his being born at Urbino has an added significance: it was the best possible point of departure for a man

Pedro Berruguete (about 1450-1504). Portrait of Duke Federico di Montefeltro and his son Guidobaldo.

Born at Paredes de Nava in Castile, Pedro Berruguete came to Italy some time before 1477. He worked at the court of Urbino where, in collaboration with the Flemish master Justus of Ghent, he painted the figures of prophets and philosophers in the duke's library. In this portrait of Federico di Montefeltro, Berruguete represents the duke reading a book and dressed in full armor, thus emphasizing his dual capacity as humanist and warrior.
Galleria Nazionale, Urbino.

Illusionist marquetry decoration in the library of Duke Federico di Montefeltro in the ducal palace of Urbino.

Painting attributed to Francesco di Giorgio Martini (1439-1502) representing an ideal city. Galleria Nazionale, Urbino.

Painting attributed to Francesco di Giorgio Martini (1439-1502) representing an ideal square. Staatliche Museen, Berlin.

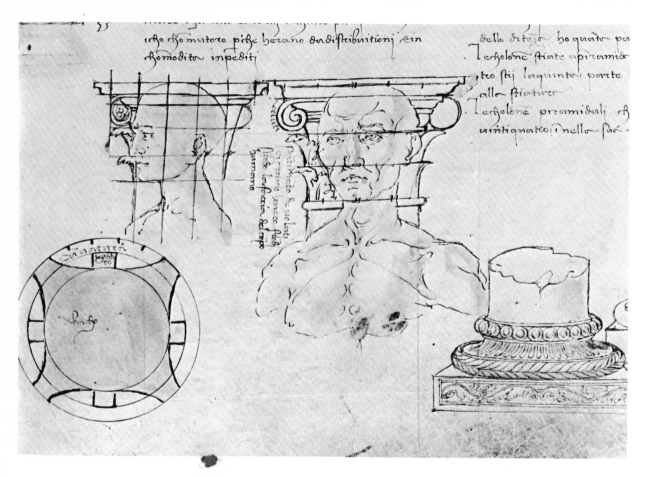

Francesco di Giorgio Martini (1439-1502).
Study of Proportions. Leaf of the Codex Saluzziano 148, folio 15 recto. Royal Library, Turin.

In 1447 the architect Matteo de' Pasti came to Rimini and began remodelling the Gothic church of San Francesco for Sigismondo Malatesta, Lord of Rimini, who wanted to convert it into a funerary monument for himself and his family. About 1450 Leon Battista Alberti redesigned the exterior in the classical style, making it one of the finest examples of Renaissance architecture. Henceforth known as the Tempio Malatestiano, the building was to be crowned with a dome over the choir, but work came to a stop after the death of Sigismondo Malatesta in 1468.

Leon Battista Alberti (about 1404-1472). The Tempio Malatestiano at Rimini.

Donato Bramante (1444-1514). Design for the Façade of Santa Maria presso San Satiro in Milan.
Cabinet des Dessins, Louvre, Paris.

This drawing is one of the first designs made by Bramante about 1479-1480 for the Renaissance church of Santa Maria which he built around the little Romanesque oratory of San Satiro. The façade is based on the structure of a Roman triumphal arch. At the same time its external design corresponds to the internal arrangement of the three-aisled nave. In his use of an ancient model and his application of the laws of proportion, Bramante shows how much he owed to the cultural milieu of Urbino and to the theories of Leon Battista Alberti.

who from earliest youth aspired to art. His father Giovanni Santi "was a painter of no great merit," wrote Vasari, "but withal a man of good understanding well qualified to guide his pupils in the right direction, which unfortunately had not been shown to himself in his youth."

His apprenticeship at Urbino was naturally complex, just as the cultural and stylistic components that entered into his art were many and complex; he completed his training at Perugia, Florence and Rome. Many were the suggestions, the ideas and promptings, that he took up and made the most of in the course of his short but strenuous career; and whether they derived from Piero della Francesca or Perugino, from Leonardo or Michelangelo, he absorbed them effortlessly and gave them an unmistakable stamp, a rhythm and harmony, of his own, moulding all he took into a style whose serene and lucid beauty remained for centuries, down to the time of Ingres and even Renoir, an unchallenged ideal.

This achievement was at once recognized and stated with rare critical acumen by Vasari. Raphael, he wrote in the 1568 edition of his *Lives of the Most Eminent Painters, Sculptors and Architects*, "was given to the world by nature when the latter, subdued by art at the hands of Michelangelo Buonarroti, resolved, with Raphael, to be subdued by art and manners together." Going beyond a purely aesthetic appreciation, beyond the antithesis between Raphael and Michelangelo, Vasari recognized the good breeding that underlies Raphael's art. "Truly," he continued, "while most artists hitherto have taken from nature something wild and strange which, besides making them abstract and fanciful, often brought out in their work the shadow and darkness of vice rather than the clarity and splendor of those virtues which make

men immortal, in Raphael on the contrary there shine forth all the rarest virtues of the soul accompanied by such grace, proficiency, beauty, modesty and fine manners as would have amply concealed any vice, however gross, and any blemish, however enormous." The art of Raphael, then, sets a moral standard, mirrors an ideal of life. In a sense, it holds up an image of the gentleman described by Castiglione, an image already overlaid, in Vasari's interpretation, with the moral doctrines of the Counter Reformation.

The ideal of "virtue" derived directly moreover from the humanistic speculations of Leon Battista Alberti, for whom "virtue" must prevail over "fortune." And Alberti's ideas and theories have their counterpart in the pictures of the greatest artist who had ever worked at Urbino, and who in fact, when visiting Urbino in 1468, had stayed with Giovanni Santi—Piero della Francesca. On the back of his portrait of Federico di Montefeltro, Piero represented the duke riding in a triumphal chariot surrounded by the four cardinal virtues. This glorification of the prince emphasized his equal merits as a leader of men (for he is portrayed with the scepter of authority) and as a pattern of moral integrity, the two capacities being inseparable. To Federico's son, Guidobaldo, Piero later dedicated his treatise on the five regular bodies.

The impersonal monumentality of Piero della Francesca's style undoubtedly left its mark on the young Raphael. In the processional banner Raphael painted in the last years of the fifteenth century for the Confraternity of Charity at Città di Castello, the composition obviously derives from Piero's *Madonna of Mercy*, the central panel of his Borgo San Sepolcro polyptych. The kinship here is not only one of theme

DIVA BAPTISTA SFORTIA VRB

◄ *Francesco Laurana (active 1453-1502).*
Marble Bust of Battista Sforza, wife of
Federico di Montefeltro and Duchess of
Urbino.
Bargello, Florence.

Supposed Self-Portrait of the Young Raphael.
Charcoal drawing.
Ashmolean Museum, Oxford.

and composition. Piero's stay at Urbino was decisive for Raphael, as were also the theories of Alberti. Donato Bramante, with whom Raphael was to be so closely associated in Rome, is said to have been a pupil of Piero's (such was the tradition recorded in 1549 by Sabba Castiglione). Bramante left Urbino some years before Raphael was born. He was working in Bergamo in 1477, and later in Milan; in 1499, after the fall of Ludovico il Moro, he moved to Rome. Whether the tradition noted by Sabba Castiglione is true or not, there can be no doubt that the influence of Piero was all-important in his formative years. This is clear from what is thought to be his earliest work, in the ducal palace at Urbino, as it so happens (the Cappella del Perdono and the architectural design of the Duke's study). It is confirmed by his work in Milan, for example the simulated apse he painted in illusionist perspective in the church of Santa Maria presso San Satiro; this might have come straight out of a picture by Piero. The consciousness of this common background catalyzed the friendship of Bramante and Raphael when they met in Rome in 1508.

Piero's influence took effect very strongly on all the artists who came to Urbino. It modified the style of the sculptor Francesco Laurana, who carved the portrait bust of Battista Sforza, Duchess of Urbino.

◀ *Raphael. Portrait of Baldassare Castiglione, 1514-1515.*

Raphael and Castiglione were close friends, and in Rome the artist painted his portrait. Castiglione was the author of "The Book of the Courtier," which not only describes the Renaissance ideal of the perfect gentleman but gives a charming picture of the court of Urbino in the time of Duke Guidobaldo di Montefeltro, whom Castiglione served as a diplomat.
Louvre, Paris.

IL LIBRO DEL CORTEGIANO
DEL CONTE BALDESAR
CASTIGLIONE.

AL DVS.

Haſſi nel priuilegio, & nella gratia ottenuta dalla Illuſtriſſima
Signoria che in queſta, ne in niun'altra Citta del ſuo
dominio ſi poſſa imprimere, ne altroue
impreſſo uendere queſto libro
del Cortegiano per·x·anni
ſotto le pene in eſſo
contenute·

Title page of "The Book of the Courtier" with the anchor and dolphin device of Aldus Manutius, the Venetian printer.

As for Alberti, his theories and practice are reflected in the architecture of Luciano Laurana and Francesco di Giorgio Martini, also in some anonymous perspective paintings. Raphael too, to begin with, adopted the spatial proportions worked out by Alberti, and though he soon modified them, the rational space composition he deduced from them remained the basis of all his later work. And not only does his use of perspective, above all in the four chambers or *stanze* he decorated in the Vatican, closely correspond to a geometric principle of spatial distribution, but his very ideal of beauty has its justification in the theories of Alberti. In a famous letter written in 1514 to Baldassare Castiglione, Raphael explains that "to paint a beautiful woman, I should want to see several beautiful women, on one condition: that your Lordship be with me to help me choose the best. But there being so few good judges and so few beautiful women, I avail myself of a certain idea that comes to mind." But already in his treatise *On Statuary* Alberti had proposed a method of arriving at ideal beauty: "It will be necessary to choose from the most beautiful bodies the most praiseworthy parts and always, to impart the utmost grace, work at them with zeal and care, difficult though it may be, because not in a single body are consummate beauties to be found, being dispersed and scarce in many bodies, and must be tirelessly sought out and learned."

According to Vasari, Giovanni Santi accompanied his son to Perugia, "where Perugino, seeing Raphael's manner of drawing and his pleasant ways, pronounced that judgment upon him which time has proved most true." It may have been so. But Giovanni Santi died in 1494, and it seems unlikely that the boy, then only eleven, had already been apprenticed to Perugino at that date. Nevertheless, Vasari's words testify to Raphael's precocity, and if he had not entered Perugino's workshop by 1494 he must have done so soon thereafter. It is safe to say that by the time he went to Perugia he was already in possession of an outlook of his own, a personal view of the world founded on an attentive study of the works he had seen at Urbino: these, reconsidered in the light of Perugino's graceful art, remained the basis on which he built for the rest of his life.

Chapter Two

At the Sources of the Renaissance

Raphael. Madonna of the Meadow, detail with Lake Trasimeno in the background, 1506. Kunsthistorisches Museum, Vienna.

A DEED executed by the notary Matteo degli Oddi on May 13, 1500, records the fact that Raphael was no longer in Urbino. This is the first indication we have that the young artist had begun his career. It does not of course mean that he entered Perugino's studio at Perugia in the year 1500. No doubt he began his apprenticeship there well before that date, for a document of December 10, 1500, refers to Raphael as a *magister* (i.e. a master painter) who, together with a fellow painter from Urbino, Evangelista di Pian di Meleto, a pupil of Giovanni Santi, has been commissioned to paint the altarpiece of the Blessed Nicholas of Tolentino for Città di Castello; this altarpiece was finished by September 13, 1501. Certainly an order from this small Umbrian town did not carry the same weight as the order for the Monteluce altarpiece which he received, shortly afterwards, from the much more important town of Perugia. But it proves that in 1500, at the age of seventeen, Raphael, having perhaps distinguished himself during his apprenticeship, and backed perhaps by Perugino, was already recognized as a fully qualified master.

So that while it is difficult to credit the date of 1494 given by Vasari for Raphael's arrival in Perugia, he may well have arrived there only a year or two later. G. B. Cavalcaselle, one of the leading Italian art historians of the nineteenth century, surmised that Raphael may have begun his training in Perugia as early as 1495, and this hypothesis has been supported more recently by Roberto Longhi, who believes that the hand of the young Raphael can be detected in one of the predella panels of Perugino's altarpiece of the Nativity, painted in 1497 for the church of Santa Maria Nuova at Fano. Another circumstance makes it seem likely that by this time Raphael had entered Perugino's studio. For in 1496, when he already had more work in hand than he could cope with, Perugino was asked to paint the audience hall in the Collegio del Cambio (chamber of commerce) at Perugia: the services of a new pupil and assistant would have been especially welcome at that time. The Cambio frescoes were finished between 1498 and 1500, and in these, particularly in the figure personifying strength, Adolfo Venturi many years ago saw the hand of Raphael. Critics today are no longer so sure about this. But whether he actually shared in the work or not, these frescoes, with which he was undoubtedly familiar, were an object lesson for the young artist from Urbino, a prime example of sound professional workmanship.

Perugino was a painter highly esteemed by Giovanni Santi who, in the *Rhymed Chronicle of*

Urbino which he wrote, mentioned him alongside Leonardo da Vinci. Perugino had probably visited Urbino; indeed the architectural setting of his *Christ Giving the Keys to St Peter* (1481) in the Sistine Chapel (which was one of the sources of Raphael's *Marriage of the Virgin*) vaguely resembles the square in front of the ducal palace at Urbino, as Adolfo Venturi pointed out. Moreover the glorification of the

Virtues in the Cambio frescoes—inspired perhaps by the humanist Maturanzio—answers, though in a less heroic vein, to the very principles which Raphael must have imbibed at the court of Urbino.

Admittedly the stages of Raphael's early development cannot be clearly traced. The sequence of his early works is unknown, and various, often contradictory datings have been proposed for them. There can be no doubt however that such masterpieces as the *Knight's Dream* and the *Three Graces* (which originally, it seems certain, formed a diptych), and also the Louvre *St Michael*, were painted shortly after the *Marriage of the Virgin*, which is signed and dated 1504. All three reflect not so much a youthful ingenuousness as a mature ability to fit the graces and charm of youth into a pictorial design that is perfectly controlled and organized thanks to a thorough grasp of the "rules" of spatial representation—rules which even then Raphael did not hesitate to break when it suited his purpose to deviate, slightly but significantly, from the perspective and proportions of Quattrocento painting.

The role of perspective in Italian Renaissance painting has been clarified by two scholars of the present day, Erwin Panofsky and Pierre Francastel. They have shown that, contrary to an academic assumption which has held the field for centuries, the representation of space in terms of perspective was

◄ *Perugino (about 1445-1523) and his Workshop.*
The Marriage of the Virgin, about 1503-1504.
Musée des Beaux-Arts, Caen.

Raphael. The Marriage of the Virgin, 1504. ►
Brera, Milan.

35

not regarded as a means of rendering visual reality or imitating nature more closely. To reduce a great stylistic (and intellectual) principle like linear perspective to a mere technical device for creating the illusion of space is to belittle and misconstrue the great adventure of Renaissance art. It is important to realize that this principle had not been erected into a hard and fast system. On the contrary, each artist handled perspective in his own way and bent it to his own purposes: Leonardo in particular departed from the canon laid down by Alberti, and so did Raphael, prompted perhaps by Leonardo's example.

Just as the architectural space of Bramante differs from that of Brunelleschi, from which it derives, so the pictorial space of Raphael differs from that of Piero della Francesca, from which it derives. If it is true that by way of Perugino Raphael harks back to Piero, he harks back to him in a spirit very different from that of his master. For in Perugino's work he glimpsed the possibilities that might be opened up by breaking (or overstepping) the "rules" laid down by Piero. Hence the eager curiosity with which he looked not only to his great Florentine contemporaries Leonardo and Michelangelo, but beyond them, back to Donatello, in the effort to work out a vision of his own—a vision which he regarded as the necessary but not immutable basis of his art.

It is important to bear these points in mind if we are to reject—as reject we must in Raphael's case— the abstract concept of genius suddenly springing into existence and following a prescribed evolution. Renaissance art was not governed by a set of fixed "rules." Being itself a structure of the mind projected in visual form, the art of the Renaissance is intimately, indivisibly, bound up with the varied and ever-changing structures of a society which,

passing in the course of centuries from medieval mysticism through the convulsions of the Reformation and the Counter Reformation, came to establish a new relationship between man and history. For the painters of the Renaissance, perspective was not a means of chronicling ephemeral appearances; it was, on the contrary, a means of possessing themselves of a space in which history could be permanently recorded. And since history comprises all past events and human activities, including artistic activity, which is a structure and not a superstructure, it was only to be expected that this representation of space by means of linear perspective should vary from one artist to another according to his own view and interpretation of the world.

Perugino, who certainly had his own way of looking at things, quite distinct from that of his predecessors, gave Raphael his first effective initiation into the art of painting. After being grounded in the rudiments by his father Giovanni Santi, Raphael found in Perugino the master best qualified to help him express all that the sensitive boy had felt and fancied during his youth in Urbino. "Perugino," wrote Lionello Venturi, "taught him a form capable of expressing, in accordance with tradition, both physical beauty and a grace instinct with deep religious faith." To Raphael, then, Perugino transmitted a conception of form, not a figural convention; a tradition with all that that term implies in the way of a historical contribution to the development of style; and beauty and grace, two components as essential to the growth of Raphael's art as the spiritual and heroic ideal he derived from Urbino.

Perugino was a great painter, greater than is commonly supposed, for his fame was eclipsed almost before he died by that of his brilliant pupil. It is

Raphael. St Michael and the Dragon. Louvre, Paris.

This small picture, datable to about 1504-1505, is thought to have been painted for the court of Urbino. Some scholars have detected a certain Flemish influence in the treatment of the background.

Raphael. The Knight's Dream, 1504-1505. National Gallery, London.

These two small panels were undoubtedly companion pieces, forming a diptych. The first illustrates an episode in the famous "Dream of Scipio" by Cicero: Scipio is shown

Raphael. The Three Graces, 1504-1505. Musée Condé, Chantilly.

asleep between Pleasure (personified by Venus) and Virtue (personified by Minerva).
The three Graces, represented in the second panel, reward the knight for choosing virtue.

true—and this will bear repeating—that by way of his master Raphael harked back to Piero della Francesca, to whom Perugino owed that geometrically ordered composition which Raphael took over, analyzing its organic components and making use of them. But already the picture space of Perugino (or better the representational purpose it served), his delightful sense of color and his use of luminous color patches mark an advance with respect to Piero. If, as Pierre Francastel has said, the artists who came after the great initiators of the Renaissance found the rules of pictorial representation largely fixed on the basis of the fundamental principles laid down by Brunelleschi (and also by Donatello), it is necessary to add that they did not assimilate those principles passively but found in them a means of enlarging and enriching their artistic outlook and resources. They accordingly embraced those principles without reserve or misgivings, each elaborating on them in his own way. Historical continuity was thus ensured, over and above such fine distinctions as those made, for example, by Leonardo, who distinguished between three types of perspective, or by Bramante in Rome who, led on by technical innovations, achieved a more resonant modulation of space than Alberti. It was to Bramante's conception of space that Raphael's art increasingly approximated, not because he imitated it but because of the historical parallel in the respective situations of the two artists.

It has generally been assumed that in the last years of the fifteenth century Perugino entered a period of crisis, either because he himself was lapsing into affectation or because he allowed his pupils too large a share in the work; and that he surmounted this crisis thanks to the infusion of a fresh vein of poetry contributed by a new pupil of genius: Raphael. Yet,

in spite of some undoubted shortcomings, Perugino at this very time was capable of painting—just before he began the Cambio frescoes in Perugia—such a masterpiece as the *Apollo and Marsyas* in the Louvre, a picture which, in the novelty of its idealization, ran counter to the conception of history dear to the early humanists or at least gave a new interpretation of it. It was a secular idealization, standing outside the pale of religious conventions: in this respect it was a suggestive precedent, one that was by no means lost on Raphael. Moreover the careful and accurate elaboration of perspective in this and subsequent works of Perugino, down to the *Marriage of the Virgin* painted (with the help of his pupils) for Perugia Cathedral about 1503-1504 and now in the Caen museum, would have shown Raphael that linear perspective was being used not as a device for reproducing visual appearances or imitating nature, but as a means of stating and defining the artist's own personal view of the world—the truth as he sees it.

Perugino's conception of space in *Christ Giving the Keys to St Peter*, and even more noticeably in his *Marriage of the Virgin*, was taken over bodily in Raphael's *Marriage of the Virgin*. In the latter we find the same taste for architectural perspective delimiting but not closing off the background, the same scale of proportion between the buildings in the background and the figures in the foreground. Yet—and the year is 1504—Raphael already reveals a different sensibility, and an unexpected readiness to break up the traditional parallelepiped of the perspective construction. He had been commissioned in 1504 to paint the *Sposalizio* or *Marriage of the Virgin* by the Albizzini family for the chapel of St Joseph in the church of San Francesco at Città di Castello, a small town in Umbria some thirty miles from Perugia. That year marks his closest adherence to the forms and methods of Perugino, and the beginning of his emancipation. The Umbrian landscape, the crystalline light bathing the softly rolling hills which surround Perugia and slope off to the west towards Lake Trasimeno (which later appears in the background of the *Madonna of the Meadow*), had become so familiar to him that he gives an accurate and evocative delineation of them in the *Marriage of the Virgin*, which in this respect is an important document.

Critics have usually praised the accurate rendering of space and architecture in this picture, while commenting unfavorably on the figures, indeed dismissing them as unconvincing puppets. Granted that this youthful work does not quite come off, that figures and setting fail to blend into a unified whole. The fact remains that it is impossible to make a sharp distinction between the good and the bad. The figures cannot be judged by quality alone, for the colors in which they are clothed are essential to the overall harmony of the composition.

In this work, and at this time, Raphael was testing out the pictorial principles, derived from Alberti, which had been handed down to him; and he was not quite satisfied with them. True, the whole composition of the *Marriage of the Virgin* obeys the laws of harmony and proportion, and above all it obeys the laws, derived from Piero della Francesca, of construction by planes. But it is built up in terms of wider intervals, such almost as to suggest a more highly colored atmosphere, and built up with a greater emphasis on the empty spaces, thrown into relief by the tiny aperture of the temple door, which leads the eye towards an illimitable horizon.

Prior to 1504 we have no certain indication that Raphael had been to Florence, but it is obvious that already in the *Marriage of the Virgin* he was abandoning the wistful grace of Perugino, the closely confined spacing of Pinturicchio's architectural settings (to which he had at first been attracted), and even the strict order of Piero della Francesca—he was abandoning these for an ambiguity that suggests the influence of Leonardo, the leading Florentine master of the day.

Vasari, in the 1568 edition of his *Lives*, refers to Pinturicchio's paintings in the library of Siena cathedral. Pinturicchio, he writes, "being a friend of Raphael's and knowing how fine a draftsman he was, took him with him to Siena, where Raphael made some preparatory drawings and cartoons for the library paintings. The reason why he did not go on with the work is as follows. While he was in Siena, some painters spoke to him with great praise of the cartoon Leonardo da Vinci had made in the hall of the pope in Florence, representing a marvellous group of horses, intended for the hall of the Palazzo; and they spoke of some nudes made in competition with Leonardo by Michelangelo Buonarroti, admirable works. Raphael was taken with so great a desire to see them, out of the love he always felt for excellence in art, that, abandoning the work at Siena and disregarding his own interests, he set out for Florence."

Vasari's account of these matters is not quite exact. The paintings in the cathedral library at Siena, illustrating the life of Aeneas Sylvius Piccolomini (Pope Pius II), were commissioned from Pinturicchio by Cardinal Francesco Todeschini Piccolomini (the future Pope Pius III) in 1502; they were executed in the course of the next four years. There is no evidence to show that Raphael had any share

◄ *Donatello (1386-1466). St George,*
carved after 1417 for the church
of Orsanmichele, Florence.
Bargello, Florence.

Raphael. Four Warriors, about ►
1504-1505. Pen drawing.
Ashmolean Museum, Oxford.

43

◀ Antonio Pollaiolo (1431/32-1498).
Hercules fighting the Hydra of
Lerna. Pen drawing illustrating
one of the Labors of Hercules.
Between 1465 and 1470 Pollaiolo
painted three large pictures on
this theme.
British Museum, London.

Raphael. Hercules fighting the ▶
Nemean Lion. Pen drawing proba-
bly made in Florence about 1505.
Royal Library, Windsor Castle.

45

Raphael. Study of Heads and Hands, with a sketch after Leonardo's Battle of Anghiari (upper left). Pen drawing of about 1504-1505. Ashmolean Museum Oxford.

The art of Leonardo and also that of Michelangelo exerted a decisive influence on Raphael during his stay in Florence. Their work not only went to shape his conception of form but encouraged him to use the drawing as a means of psychological investigation. This influence is attested by the sketch copied from the Battle of Anghiari in the upper left corner and by the two head studies: the features of the old man are typically Leonardesque, while the young man, despite the supple modelling, is reminiscent of Michelangelo.

Leonardo da Vinci (1452-1519). Detail of a pen drawing representing the Battle of the Standard. Preparatory study for the Battle of Anghiari, a mural painting ordered in May 1504 by the gonfalier Pier Soderini for the Hall of the Great Council in the Palazzo Vecchio, Florence. The painting itself soon fell to pieces, the colors having been forced to dry too rapidly by the application of heat. It was, nevertheless, a work of the highest importance in the further development of Renaissance art, for it exerted a profound influence on the young Raphael and on Michelangelo as well. British Museum, London. ▼

in them. It was in 1504 that Leonardo and Michelangelo were invited to paint frescoes illustrating episodes from Florentine history in the Hall of the Great Council in the Palazzo Vecchio. Leonardo drew the preliminary sketch representing the *Battle of Anghiari*, and went on to execute the central part of his fresco, the *Battle of the Standard*; this fresco rapidly deteriorated and was later destroyed. Late in 1504 Michelangelo began his preliminary sketch representing the *Battle of Cascina*; the actual painting was never executed.

A letter from Giovanna Feltria della Rovere recommending the painter to Pier Soderini, head of the Florentine government, shows that Raphael must have been in Florence in the last few months of 1504. Whether this was his first visit, or whether he had been there before with Perugino, who was highly esteemed in Florence, does not greatly matter. What is certain is that from this time, late 1504, his work shows the unmistakable imprint and clarity of Florentine art, and by this influence it was permanently marked.

Raphael reached Florence at a time of ferment and change in Florentine art, a time when, thanks to Leonardo and Michelangelo, it was being given a momentous reorientation. A few years later it fell to Michelangelo and Raphael himself, in a new and splendid metamorphosis, to make Rome instead of Florence the focal point of European art. "It is to the decade of Julius II's energetic pontificate (1503-1513) that the decisive evolution must be assigned; it was then that Florentine culture emigrated, losing its narrowness and becoming one of the essential components of Roman culture" (André Chastel). The change taking place was due to the rapid growth toward maturity. The traditions of the immediate past were overthrown, as a further stage in the evolving structure of artistic language was attained. The splendid serenity and assurance of Quattrocento art broke down, the confident assumption that art and science were one fell to the ground, in the face of other imperatives. The golden rule of the Quattrocento masters of perspective painting gave place to the anxious experimentation which impelled, along different paths, the two great creators of the High Renaissance: Leonardo and Michelangelo. Raphael found them both before him, as examples and points of comparison, at the moment when this reorientation of art entered what was perhaps its most decisive phase.

His three small early pictures, the *Knight's Dream*, the *Three Graces* and *St Michael*, must have been painted in 1504-1505. They can scarcely be dated any earlier because they reflect so clearly his dissatisfaction with conventional settings, his striving after a more fanciful and poetic handling of space and a color magic deriving not only from the Flemish masters (as in his *St Michael*) but also from the moody and suggestive ambiguity of Leonardo, which he reinterprets with a sure touch. Without losing his balance, he assimilated all that appealed to him in the Florentine art world, discovering horizons unsuspected at Perugia and psychological subtleties alien to his early training. Yet, with a critical acuity whose vigilance was seldom to be relaxed, he scrutinized the work of the masters who came within his ken, and looked back inquiringly over the whole course of Florentine art during the previous century.

Raphael. The Granduca Madonna, 1504-1505. ►
Pitti Palace, Florence.

◄ *Leonardo da Vinci (1452-1519). Studies for the Battle of Anghiari. Pen drawing with annotations written backwards in Leonardo's characteristic manner. Accademia, Venice.*

Michelangelo (1475-1564). Pen Drawing of Men Fighting, 1505. Preparatory study for the Battle of Cascina, a painting ordered by the gonfalier Pier Soderini for the Hall of the Great Council in the Palazzo Vecchio, Florence. Ashmolean Museum, Oxford.

The art of Leonardo and also that of Michelangelo exerted a decisive influence on Raphael during his stay in Florence. Their work not only went to shape his conception of form but encouraged him to use the drawing as a means of psychological investigation. This influence is attested by the sketch copied from the Battle of Anghiari in the upper left corner and by the two head studies: the features of the old man are typically Leonardesque, while the young man, despite the supple modelling, is reminiscent of Michelangelo.

Leonardo da Vinci (1452-1519). Detail of a pen drawing representing the Battle of the Standard. Preparatory study for the Battle of Anghiari, a mural painting ordered in May 1504 by the gonfalier Pier Soderini for the Hall of the Great Council in the Palazzo Vecchio, Florence. The painting itself soon fell to pieces, the colors having been forced to dry too rapidly by the application of heat. It was, nevertheless, a work of the highest importance in the further development of Renaissance art, for it exerted a profound influence on the young Raphael and on Michelangelo as well. British Museum, London. ▼

in them. It was in 1504 that Leonardo and Michelangelo were invited to paint frescoes illustrating episodes from Florentine history in the Hall of the Great Council in the Palazzo Vecchio. Leonardo drew the preliminary sketch representing the *Battle of Anghiari,* and went on to execute the central part of his fresco, the *Battle of the Standard;* this fresco rapidly deteriorated and was later destroyed. Late in 1504 Michelangelo began his preliminary sketch representing the *Battle of Cascina;* the actual painting was never executed.

A letter from Giovanna Feltria della Rovere recommending the painter to Pier Soderini, head of the Florentine government, shows that Raphael must have been in Florence in the last few months of 1504. Whether this was his first visit, or whether he had been there before with Perugino, who was highly esteemed in Florence, does not greatly matter. What is certain is that from this time, late 1504, his work shows the unmistakable imprint and clarity of Florentine art, and by this influence it was permanently marked.

Raphael reached Florence at a time of ferment and change in Florentine art, a time when, thanks to Leonardo and Michelangelo, it was being given a momentous reorientation. A few years later it fell to Michelangelo and Raphael himself, in a new and splendid metamorphosis, to make Rome instead of Florence the focal point of European art. "It is to the decade of Julius II's energetic pontificate (1503-1513) that the decisive evolution must be assigned; it was then that Florentine culture emigrated, losing its narrowness and becoming one of the essential components of Roman culture" (André Chastel). The change taking place was due to the rapid growth toward maturity. The traditions of the immediate past were overthrown, as a further stage in the evolving structure of artistic language was attained. The splendid serenity and assurance of Quattrocento art broke down, the confident assumption that art and science were one fell to the ground, in the face of other imperatives. The golden rule of the Quattrocento masters of perspective painting gave place to the anxious experimentation which impelled, along different paths, the two great creators of the High Renaissance: Leonardo and Michelangelo. Raphael found them both before him, as examples and points of comparison, at the moment when this reorientation of art entered what was perhaps its most decisive phase.

His three small early pictures, the *Knight's Dream,* the *Three Graces* and *St Michael,* must have been painted in 1504-1505. They can scarcely be dated any earlier because they reflect so clearly his dissatisfaction with conventional settings, his striving after a more fanciful and poetic handling of space and a color magic deriving not only from the Flemish masters (as in his *St Michael*) but also from the moody and suggestive ambiguity of Leonardo, which he reinterprets with a sure touch. Without losing his balance, he assimilated all that appealed to him in the Florentine art world, discovering horizons unsuspected at Perugia and psychological subtleties alien to his early training. Yet, with a critical acuity whose vigilance was seldom to be relaxed, he scrutinized the work of the masters who came within his ken, and looked back inquiringly over the whole course of Florentine art during the previous century.

Raphael. The Granduca Madonna, 1504-1505. ▶
Pitti Palace, Florence.

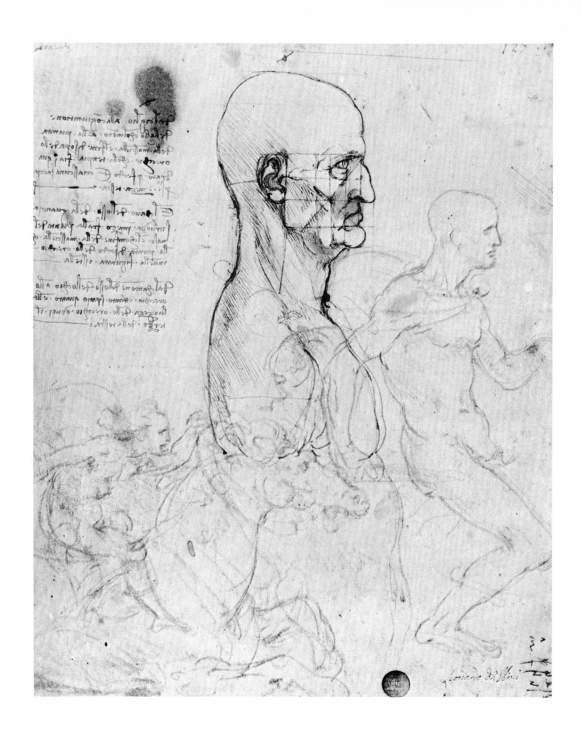

Leonardo da Vinci (1452-1519). The Virgin and Child with St Anne and St John the Baptist. Charcoal heightened with white lead. Preparatory study for the Louvre picture of the Virgin and Child with St Anne, painted by Leonardo after his return to Florence in 1500. National Gallery, London.

Raphael. The Virgin and Child with St John the Baptist.
Preparatory sketch for the Esterhazy Madonna in the Museum of Fine Arts, Budapest,
painted between 1505 and 1507. Print Room, Uffizi, Florence.

PAGE 54: *Raphael. Madonna of the Goldfinch (Virgin and Child with the Boy St John), about 1507. Uffizi, Florence.* ▶

PAGE 55: *Raphael. Madonna of the Meadow (Virgin and Child with the Boy St John), 1506. Kunsthistorisches Museum, Vienna.* ▶

54

Raphael. Figure studies for the right side of the Entombment.

56

Pen drawings.
British Museum,
London.

Vasari can be relied on when he tells us that Raphael, "this most excellent painter," as he calls him, "studied in the city of Florence the old things of Masaccio, and all that he saw in the works of Leonardo and Michelangelo caused him to attend even more eagerly to his studies, and thus to make extraordinary progress in his art and his manner." And while in Florence, Vasari adds, Raphael was "on familiar terms with Fra Bartolomeo of the convent of San Marco, whose color pleasing him much, he sought to imitate it, while in return he taught the good father perspective."

The references here are quite precise. For Raphael, Masaccio was the pathfinder; he saw in Leonardo and Michelangelo the men who, having pursued that path as far as it would go, had branched off on another; he was attracted to Fra Bartolomeo because the latter turned to account, though within a narrower compass, the spatial and coloristic lessons of Leonardo.

Nor is it Raphael's paintings alone that testify to these influences, which he quickly assimilated and transformed: a look at his drawings of this period will show that they contain direct "quotations" from the Florentine masters. In one of them there reappears, with a very slight difference in the pose that almost passes unnoticed, the St George of Donatello. In another, the movement of the figure, so much more complex than hitherto in its anatomical structure, reveals how intently he had studied the works of Verrocchio and Antonio Pollaiolo. Still other drawings reflect the dynamic sweep of Leonardo's studies for the *Battle of Anghiari*. Raphael in fact found himself confronted by an immense repertory of forms which he explored and examined with great discernment.

His study of Florentine art bore fruitful results. First of all, as is evident in the *Marriage of the Virgin* and even more in the *Knight's Dream*, the *Three Graces* and *St Michael*, it gave him a firmer and more sensitive grasp of the technique of spatial representation, such as went well beyond that of Piero della Francesca which, nevertheless, even more than that of Perugino, remained his indispensable point of departure. It was of course from Leonardo in the first place that he acquired this deeper insight and refinement which shows itself above all, by way of a heightening of color values, in the landscape backgrounds of his figure paintings on both religious and secular themes.

It was in Florence, too, that he learned to render the movements of the human body with greater ease, recording physical action from the slightest to the most strenuous with deft and accurate linework. His Madonnas, instead of lay figures standing for abstract religious values, are living, tangible presences, so appealing in their natural grace and charm that they became for centuries the ideal of human beauty.

Their beauty and grace is not the effect of mere technical mastery in the handling of forms: it comes of psychological insight. Raphael's ideal of beauty would never have commanded the allegiance of so many generations to come, had it been a mere formal

Raphael. The Entombment of Christ, 1507, ordered by ▶ *Atalanta Baglioni in memory of her son Grifonetto for the chapel of the Baglioni family in the church of San Francesco al Prato, Perugia.*
The picture is signed and dated: "Raphael Urbinas M.D.VII"
Borghese Gallery, Rome.

Raphael. Portrait of Maddalena Doni, about 1506. Pitti Palace, Florence.

device. To be sure, his psychology has not the depth and complexity of Leonardo's; it is simpler and more popular, but no less effective for that.

From the *Granduca Madonna* to the *Madonna of the Goldfinch*, from the *Madonna of the Meadow* to the *Esterhazy Madonna*, all painted between 1505 and 1507, Raphael can be seen absorbing the lesson of Leonardo, profiting by it in a critical, not a merely passive spirit. And this, be it remembered, was the restless and perturbing Leonardo of the first years of the Cinquecento, the master who had just created the *St Anne* cartoon, the *Leda* (which Raphael copied in a drawing), the *Mona Lisa*. Here again we find a "quotation": Raphael's portrait of *Maddalena Doni*, dating to about 1506, is a masterpiece born of a masterpiece, for it could never have been painted without a knowledge of the *Mona Lisa*.

The placing and the pose of the figure in Raphael's famous portrait, the melting softness of the color shadings, the mysterious simplicity of the landscape, the use of certain accessories as emblems—all this derives from Leonardo. Perspective, which in Leonardo's hands was not only linear but at once a matter "of line, of color, of position" (to use his own words), now loosened and mellowed the geometric rigor with which Raphael had applied the principles of Alberti. So much so that the landscape stretching behind the figure ceases to be a framework, a limiting background: it reflects and enhances, in an unbroken continuity of movement, the grace and beauty enveloping the figure in the foreground. It is an earthbound figure, however, perfectly at home in this world, alluding to nothing beyond or above itself. Starting out from a composition taken over from Leonardo, Raphael had the genius to create on that basis an entirely new type of portrait which he instinctively attuned to feelings and thoughts common to all mankind, yet raised to a sublime perfection and serenity.

Between 1504 and 1508 Raphael did not reside continuously in Florence. He was often absent, revisiting Urbino and working in Perugia. It was a noblewoman of Perugia, Atalanta Baglioni, who ordered from him an *Entombment of Christ* for the church of San Francesco al Prato in Perugia, in memory of her son Grifonetto who had been killed in one of the feuds that divided the city into rival factions. Signed and dated 1507, this picture is now in the Borghese Gallery, Rome. Though somewhat lacking in unity, it is a work of great power. Its elaborate monumentality, kept under perfect control, is more complex than anything he had attempted before, for he was impelled by different intentions —intentions by no means antagonistic to his earlier aims, but complementing them rather. Here the impact of Michelangelo is plain to see not only in the general design of the picture, but in its surging energy, the torsion of the bodies and, most strikingly of all, in the "quotations" made directly, with no attempt to gloss them over, from the great Florentine. The figure of the dead Christ is obviously inspired by Michelangelo's sculpture. The figure of the kneeling woman on the right is directly derived from the Doni *Madonna*. The debt to Michelangelo appears even more clearly in the preliminary sketches: the figures arise out of an intricate play of flickering lines which, however much they still owe to Leonardo, are imbued with a restrained and mournful monumentality. Here again, then, Raphael draws on several sources of inspiration, combining and adapting them to suit his own purposes. Thus the dramatic severity of Michelangelo, dissolved in a lyrical synthesis, takes on more tender accents, no less lofty than his. The landscape sloping up gently behind the figures, which seems known and familiar, in no way mysterious, is like an echo of his own feelings. Intent on communicating directly, Raphael here has succeeded in recording images and sentiments which proved to have a universal appeal. It is this that distinguishes him from the masters whom he studied so carefully and searchingly. It is this that distinguishes him above all from the Michelangelo of the Vatican frescoes.

In the space of a very few years Raphael had developed his powers to the full, thanks in large part to his ability to learn from others, choosing from them with rare critical insight all that served his turn. He had mastered all the resources needed to express in painting—which for him was a means of exploring and knowing reality—the role he was called on to play in contemporary history. Not only Perugia but Florence itself had become too narrow for him: he was ready to move on to the wider stage of Rome and the papal court of Julius II.

Chapter Three

The Remaking of Rome

Raphael. *The School of Athens, 1509-1510.*
Stanza della Segnatura, Vatican Palace.

LATE in the year 1508 Raphael went to Rome, where he was to spend the rest of his life. "And this came about," writes Vasari, "because Bramante of Urbino, who was in the service of Pope Julius II, and being distantly related to Raphael and a native of the same parts, wrote to him that he had been using his influence with the Pope to obtain leave for Raphael to display his powers in certain rooms of the palace."

Vasari here gives a trustworthy account of this event (apart from the fact that Bramante was not actually related to Raphael). Great things were going forward in Rome, great projects were afoot. And Bramante, the leading architect of the day (though in Lombardy he had also worked as a painter), had every reason to bring his young countryman to Rome, not only out of a sense of loyalty, which one native of Urbino would naturally feel for another, but because he also needed support. The Rome of 1508, so avid of novelty, of variety and contrast, had already fallen under the spell of Michelangelo, who on the 10th of May had begun painting his frescoes on the ceiling of the Sistine Chapel. Bramante too stood for change and renewal; he too was an avant-garde artist. But his cultural position was quite a different one from that of Michelangelo, and he was no doubt eager to enlist the support of his young friend. If such were Bramante's motives, Raphael, for his part, certainly had hopes and expectations of his own.

He came to Rome, then, at the very time when Julius II, with his willful impetuosity, had resolved to set his artists to work renovating the Vatican palace and rebuilding St Peter's. A letter is extant purporting to have been written by Raphael from Rome, on September 5, 1508, to the Bolognese painter Francesco Francia; most historians regard it, on good grounds, as a forgery. But there is also a document of January 13, 1509, which records a payment made for work being done by Raphael in the room which came to be called the Stanza della Segnatura because in this room the pope heard appeals and signed pardons. Julius II had decided to reserve these chambers for his own use, for he refused to live any longer in the Borgia apartments which, he said, brought to mind the "foul and villainous memory" of Alexander VI, his predecessor. In the rooms or *stanze* chosen by Julius, some of the walls had already been decorated by Piero della Francesca, Bartolomeo della Gatta, Luca Signorelli, and Bramantino, as we know from Vasari; and at that moment Perugino was still working in them, together with Sodoma, Baldassare Peruzzi, and Lorenzo Lotto. Raphael does not seem

Above: *The Virtues. Justinian Receiving the Pandects. Gregory IX Receiving the Decretals.*

Left: *The School of Athens.*

Below: *Parnassus.*

Right: *The Dispute over the Holy Sacrament.*

Above: *The Mass of Bolsena.*

Left: *Heliodorus Driven from the Temple.*

Below: *St Peter Delivered from Prison by the Angel.*

Right: *The Meeting of Leo the Great and Attila.*

1. STANZA DI ELIODORO.

Above   *The Mass of Bolsena.*

Right   *The Meeting of Leo the Great and Attila.*

Below   *St Peter Delivered from Prison by the Angel.*

Left   *Heliodorus Driven from the Temple.*

The decoration in grisaille along the base of the wall, beneath Raphael's frescoes, is attributed to Perino del Vaga working from designs provided by Raphael. Eleven caryatids symbolize Commerce, Religion, Law, Peace, Patronage, Nobility, Navigation, Abundance, Stock-breeding, Agriculture, and Vine-growing.
Beside the windows are painted four herms, and below, among the figures, are several scenes referring to the good government of the Papal States.

2. STANZA DELLA SEGNATURA.

Above   *The Virtues, in the lunette, and on either side of the window, the Emperor Justinian Receiving the Pandects from Trebonianus, and Pope Gregory IX (with the features of Pope Julius II) Receiving the Decretals from St Raymond of Penafort.*

Right   *The Dispute over the Holy Sacrament.*

Below   *Parnassus.*

Under this composition, Alexander the Great Having Homer's Poems Placed in the Tomb of Achilles, and Augustus Saving the Manuscript of Virgil's Aeneid from the Fire. These two scenes are thought to have been painted by Perino del Vaga.

Left   *The School of Athens.*

The monochrome decoration on the base of the wall was executed by Perino del Vaga at a later period, during the pontificate of Paul III.

3. STANZA DELL'INCENDIO.

Above   *The Burning of the Borgo.*

Right   *The Crowning of Charlemagne.*

Below   *The Justification of Leo III.*

Left   *The Battle of Ostia.*

On the base of the wall are caryatids and figures representing Charlemagne, Aistulf, Godfrey of Bouillon, Lothair I and Ferdinand the Catholic, painted by Giulio Romano.

CEILING OF THE STANZA DI ELIODORO.

Arranged around a medallion with the arms of Julius II are four scenes corresponding to the frescoes on the side walls and representing the Sacrifice of Isaac, the Lord Appearing to Noah, Jacob's Ladder, and the Burning Bush. These paintings are attributed to Baldassare Peruzzi.

CEILING OF THE STANZA DELLA SEGNATURA.

Thirteen compartments are arranged in a setting of grotesques. In the center, an octagon with angels holding the pope's coat of arms. In the tondi, each figure corresponds to the frescoes on the side walls: Justice, Theology, Poetry, and Philosophy. In the corners, Adam and Eve, Apollo and Marsyas, Astronomy, the Judgment of Solomon.
These ceiling decorations are generally attributed to Raphael, but Apollo and Marsyas is probably by Sodoma and Baldassare Peruzzi, and Adam and Eve by Sodoma.
Between Julius II's coat of arms, the tondi, and the main scenes, there are four compartments, each with two scenes on historical and mythological subjects.

CEILING OF THE STANZA DELL'INCENDIO

The tondi contain religious scenes on the theme of the Trinity: these had been painted by Perugino in 1507 and Raphael left them untouched.

Above: *Ceiling of the Stanza di Eliodoro.*

Middle: *Ceiling of the Stanza della Segnatura.*

Below: *Ceiling of the Stanza dell'Incendio.*

Above: *The Burning of the Borgo.*

Left: *The Battle of Ostia.*

Below: *The Justification of Leo III.*

Right: *The Crowning of Charlemagne.*

71

Portrait of Julius II. Pencil drawing.

This drawing is not by Raphael. It is probably a study for the portrait in the Uffizi, an early copy of Raphael's portrait of Julius II.
Devonshire Collections, Chatsworth.

74

to have been overawed by the work of so many illustrious predecessors. He set to work with serene confidence, painting "in so delicate and sweet a manner," writes Vasari, "that Pope Julius caused all the pictures of the other masters, both ancient and modern, to be destroyed, that Raphael might have the sole credit for all the works here performed down to the present time."

His success was therefore immediate. Julius II saw in Raphael the ideal interpreter of the triumph of the Church in the age of humanism, the man whose art could best justify the spiritual power in its concerted effort, under Julius, to renew and reconfirm the grandeur of Rome. Julius was a fighting pope, a shrewd politician who in these years of strife dominated the political scene in Italy and in Europe as a whole. He was the nephew of Sixtus IV (1471-1484), the pope who had opened the Capitoline Museum, the first public museum in Europe, thus giving the people at large their first opportunity of freely enjoying works of art. Julius II was equally art-minded, with spectacular results, for he had the good fortune to secure the services of some of the very greatest artists of the Renaissance (having had the discernment to recognize them as such): Bramante, whom he entrusted with his grandiose project of rebuilding St Peter's; Michelangelo, whom he summoned to Rome to carve his tomb, and then commanded to paint the ceiling of the Sistine Chapel; and Raphael, who painted for him the mighty picture-poem in the Vatican Stanze, mirroring in its imagery the doctrines of the triumphant Neo-Platonism of the Church of Rome, and so thanks to its ideological content answering better than any other work to the pope's own aims and ideals. For this warrior pope was fully alive to the dangers of the times, to the troubled spirits of his contemporaries, to the gathering storm that threatened to shake the absolute authority of the Roman popes. He needed a demonstrative glorification of the power of the Church and papacy, a reaffirmation of both its spiritual and political pre-eminence, and of its high cultural mission as well. If with Michelangelo, who was and remained a troubled spirit, he came into sharp conflict, with Raphael he was obviously at his ease and could confidently entrust him, as the humanist historian Paolo Giovio has recorded, with the frescoes in the Vatican Stanze, whose general plan and subjects he himself had chosen, probably in consultation with the scholars of the papal court.

It was thus the will of Julius II, a radical and even an iconoclast, that the power of the Church should be identified with a demonstration of the revived power of Rome, the city whose grandiose heritage he coveted and which, by linking the present to the past, he meant to reaffirm as the perennial center and motive force of history. Thus the new St Peter's would take the place of the old Constantinian basilica: it was to stand for the historical presence of the Church, bringing that presence to the attention of all mankind. Thus the Sistine frescoes would be a Biblical document illustrating the continuity between the Old Testament and the New. Thus the paintings in the

PAGE 76: *Raphael. The School of Athens, detail: Aristotle,* ▶
1509-1510.
Stanza della Segnatura, Vatican Palace.

PAGE 77: *Raphael. Preparatory Drawing for the School of* ▶
Athens, detail of the portraits of Zoroaster and Ptolemy,
1509. Ambrosiana, Milan.

ETIC

Stanze, with their harmonious, all-enveloping distribution of spaces and the thematic division of the scenes, would demonstrate, in the most vivid and intelligible terms, the cultural and ideological legacy, the Neo-Platonic ideal, which the pope was conscious of having received from antiquity and meant to revive in the present.

Of all this, Raphael is quite obviously not a passive interpreter, he is not a docile instrument in the hands of the pope. The Vatican Stanze, and the Stanza della Segnatura in particular which he decorated between 1508 and 1511, represent the happiest outcome of his aims and aspirations. His long apprenticeship; the culture in which he had steeped himself at Urbino; all that he had learned at Perugia and Florence; his intense study of Leonardo and Michelangelo, who continued to influence him, more so than ever in Rome—all this was combined in a perfect synthesis, determining the terms and structures of an artistic language which expressed on the highest plane that glorification desired by the pope. In close contact with Julius II, at a court still more refined than that of Urbino, more cultured and above all more *modern*, Raphael underwent a change, adjusted himself to his new surroundings, and began a new line of development whose basis, undoubtedly, had been laid before but which he now followed with a self-assurance, an unsuspected ease of handling, and a cultural enrichment that charmed and conquered not only the aristocracy of Rome and the intellectual élite but

◄ *Raphael. Preparatory Drawing for the School of Athens, detail showing a boy handing to Pythagoras a tablet on which (in the fresco in the Stanza della Segnatura) Raphael has carefully represented the musical scale of Pythagoras. Ambrosiana, Milan.*

also the people, because it was conveyed with such luminous clarity. The themes illustrated in the frescoes in the Stanza della Segnatura, in the *Disputa*, the *School of Athens*, the *Parnassus*, the figures personifying the Virtues, unfold with an effortless simplicity and naturalness, such is the tact and apparent spontaneity with which he handles them. Yet they were all highly complex themes, whose interpretation was in fact very carefully prepared and worked out, as is proved by the large number of preliminary studies and cartoons which he made.

The True, the Good, and the Beautiful were the subjects set by Julius II for the Stanza della Segnatura: these were the ideals of Neo-Platonic philosophy. The True, in its theological sense as revealed truth, is the theme of the *Disputa*, or *Dispute over the Holy Sacrament*. (This, the traditional title, is not quite accurate: the fresco actually represents the Triumph of the Eucharist.) The True in its natural and rational sense is the theme of the *School of Athens*, which stands for philosophy. The Good, identified with the theological and cardinal virtues and with civil and canon law, is symbolized in two frescoes painted by Raphael's assistants: *Pope Gregory IX Receiving the Decretals* and *Trebonianus Presenting the Pandects to the Emperor Justinian*. The Beautiful is the theme of *Mount Parnassus*, in which it is identified with poetry and music. Figures personifying the True (*Theology* and *Philosophy*), the Good (*Justice*) and the Beautiful (*Poetry*) appear above these scenes in the vaulting, in the corners of which are represented the Prime Movement (*Astronomy*), the *Judgment of Solomon*, *Adam and Eve*, and *Apollo and Marsyas*. There are still other scenes, both historical (in monochrome) and mythological (in color), but none of these are by Raphael.

Raphael. Parnassus, 1510-1511. Stanza della Segnatura, Vatican Palace.

Raphael. The Dispute over the Holy Sacrament, 1509. Stanza della Segnatura, Vatican Palace.

Raphael. The School of Athens, detail of the background architecture, 1509-1510. Stanza della Segnatura, Vatican Palace.

Donato Bramante (1444-1514). Apse of the Church of Santa Maria del Popolo, Rome, 1505-1509.

The Laocoon, detail. Pio-Clementino Museum, Vatican City.

Raphael. Study of Heads for the Parnassus. Pencil drawing, 1510. Royal Library, Windsor Castle.

The Laocoon is a Hellenistic sculpture of the second century B.C., discovered in Rome on January 14, 1506. It was recognized at once as the marble described by Pliny as the work of the Rhodian sculptors Athenodorus, Agesander, and Polydorus.
Bought by Pope Julius II, the Laocoon was placed in the so-called Court of Statues of the Belvedere Palace, where several other ancient marbles had already been collected. This discovery aroused the keenest interest among the painters and sculptors who were then working in Rome. Raphael clearly took inspiration from it for his portrait of Homer in the Parnassus fresco.

This complex scheme of symbolism and ideology imposed by Julius II might have led another artist astray in the labyrinths of philosophical and literary interpretation. Not so with Raphael. He mastered the themes imposed on him, transmuted them into pictorial terms, and made them the vehicle of his personal contribution to the development of the humanistic ideals. The elaborate symbolism is kept under control. The archaeological references, the "quotations" (for example, the features of Homer in the *Parnassus*, which were obviously suggested by those of Laocoön in the famous piece of antique sculpture discovered in Rome in 1506), are given a present relevance. The figures grouped around Apollo are those of famous poets, writers and musicians, not only of the past, but also of Raphael's time. In the *School of Athens*, Plato resembles Leonardo, Euclid resembles Bramante; the figure of Heraclitus, inserted as an afterthought, is a portrait of Michelangelo; Zoroaster seems to be intended to represent the humanist scholar Pietro Bembo. Bramante also figures in the *Disputa*, and Raphael himself appears, together with Sodoma, in the *School of Athens*. A figure in the *Parnassus* has recently been identified with Michelangelo.

These portrait details are significant not only as evidence of Raphael's wonderful skill as an illustrator. More importantly, they reflect his profound awareness of the Renaissance tradition, that tradition whose rudiments he had been initiated into during his childhood at Urbino, and whose conceptions he had familiarized himself with and mastered during the busy, thoughtful, inquisitive years of his apprenticeship and young manhood. In Raphael, the spirit of the Renaissance and its conception of the artist's function found their highest embodiment. A temple of fame awaited philosophers and artists, a place worthy of them, where they should be seen to be the equal of the great ones of the earth. Their presence there vouched for the continuity of history and the continuity of the search for the True, the Good, and the Beautiful: philosophers and artists inquire on a par into the higher categories of the human spirit. Classical thought, Roman Christianity, and the long historical tradition connected with them are valid in so far as they apply to the present. Like Julius II, Raphael in his painting embarked on a *renovatio Romae*, a remaking of Rome, and to this a decisive contribution was made by the contemporary artists and scholars, and musicians, whom he represented here and there. With the utmost simplicity, and also with perfect assurance, Raphael asserted the primacy of art in the making of a civilization. He had begun work in the Stanza della Segnatura almost as soon as he had arrived in Rome, "before he had yet gained full authority," as Paolo Giovio wrote—that is, before his art commanded the full respect and admiration of a pope, a court, and a city engrossed

Raphael. Parnassus, detail: A Poet, 1510-1511. ▶

Raphael represents Apollo on Mount Parnassus surrounded by the Graces, the Muses, the Greek and Latin poets of antiquity, and even some contemporary poets. It has not been possible to identify all the figures with certainty, but the following can be recognized: Sappho (holding a scroll with her name on it), Alcaeus, Anacreon, Corinna, Homer (with his characteristic features), Horace, Ennius, Ovid, Propertius, Statius, Tibullus, Virgil, together with Dante (easily recognizable), Petrarch, Boccaccio, perhaps Ariosto, Tebaldeo (with the features of Michelangelo, according to a recent hypothesis), and Sannazzaro.
Stanza della Segnatura, Vatican Palace.

Raphael. The Mass of Bolsena, 1512. Stanza di Eliodoro, Vatican Palace.

in the quest for a new grandeur. But he very quickly imposed his authority on them and took the lead in that quest for grandeur.

The fact is that Raphael moved easily in the most highly cultured circles of Renaissance Rome, which took him up, moreover, with unfeigned warmth and sympathy. The style of his painting answered to contemporary trends in literature and music. Above all, the space composition of the frescoes in the Stanza della Segnatura has a musical harmony in the majestic ordering of the picture elements, in the carefully studied proportions and relationships, almost mathematical in their precision, which seems to correspond to the experiments of contemporary composers. Think, for example, of the new sonorities of a musician like Josquin des Prez, or the musical analogies suggested by a theorist like Leon Battista Alberti in his discussion of ideal proportions: "These selfsame numbers, to be sure, which bring it about that the harmony of voices is exceedingly pleasant to the ears of men, are the very numbers which also give such wonderful pleasure to both eyes and mind."

Many scholars, among them a great historian of architecture, Rudolf Wittkower, have stressed the importance of the relationship between music and architecture during the Renaissance, the more so since this close relationship corresponds to the Neo-Platonic ideal. Needless to say, music occupied a place of honor at the papal court. For musicians, as for painters and architects, Rome was a center of attraction, holding out the promise of recognition and fame, for it was quick to welcome innovation, though never uncritically. Pope Leo X (1513-1521), nephew of Lorenzo the Magnificent and successor of Julius II, was himself a composer who, in his boyhood in Florence, had studied under the musician

Heinrich Isaac. Raphael gave due prominence to music among the other arts in the *speculum doctrinale* of his Segnatura frescoes. It has even been suggested that Apollo, in the *Parnassus*, may be a portrait of the musician Giacomo Sansecondo (who is also mentioned by Castiglione in his *Book of the Courtier*). A more precise reference is to be found in the *School of Athens* "on the tablet facing the figure of Pythagoras... He gave here in an ingenious diagrammatic design of the four strings of the ancient lyra the whole system of the Pythagorean harmonic scale. This representation is interwoven with and expressive of Raphael's complex programme; however, it must suffice here to say that above the teacher Pythagoras appears the heroic figure of the great pupil carrying the *Timaeus* in one hand and pointing upward with the other. This is Raphael's interpretation of the harmony of the universe which Plato described in the *Timaeus* on the basis of Pythagoras' discovery of the ratios of musical consonances" (Wittkower). It is worth recalling and emphasizing this interpretation of Wittkower's because it seems more correct and penetrating than the traditional, oversimplified interpretation of the *School of Athens*, which sees it as drawing a contrast beween materialism (Aristotle) and idealism (Plato). On the tablet of Pythagoras, moreover, Raphael has inscribed in Greek characters the words diatessaron, diapente, and diapason, which are the musical intervals of a fourth, a fifth and an eighth; and beside them he has added the Greek word for tone.

The French art historian Pierre Francastel, referring to the studies made by the American musicologist Lowinsky, has emphasized the close correspondence between space composition in music and in painting. "The Renaissance," he writes in this connection, "had the sense of measure, but it also had a sense of the infinite." Already in Raphael's early *Marriage of the Virgin*, over and above the influence of Perugino we feel this aspiration toward an infinite space. Even more precise and, by now, fully achieved, is the space effect in the Segnatura frescoes. First of all because space here is not only the locus and setting of the scenes represented, the place where the action unfolds; it is a space which projects out beyond the picture into the center of the room, a space which seems to envelope the spectator himself. Secondly because in the Segnatura frescoes, above all in the *School of Athens*, the space effect is continually shifting and changing, like an echo ceaselessly reverberating. In order to convey this resonance of space, to make its infinite continuity perceptible in the harmony of the proportional relationships (each scene has a definite center and focal point of its own, and in effect its proportional mean), Raphael turned for guidance to the foremost master of space composition then to be found in Rome, and the one whose work was most congenial to him: Bramante.

The mighty vaults overarching the figures in Raphael's *School of Athens* have been thought by some scholars to be modeled on the vaults designed by Bramante for the new St Peter's, then under construction. But apart from the actual forms there is a deeper parallel in the quality of the space and the mathematical ratio of the proportions. Already in 1502 or thereabouts Bramante had built in Rome one of the masterpieces of Renaissance architecture, the small temple in the cloister of San Pietro in Montorio; its design is based on the ancient Roman temple of the Tiburtine Sibyl, though with a different spatial arrangement, whose effect, in the harmonic propor-

tion of the orders, is almost musical. Between 1505 and 1509 Bramante had built the choir of the church of Santa Maria del Popolo (the same church in which Raphael, working as an architect, was soon to build the Chigi Chapel). The curvature of the space, the junction between the bowl-shaped vault and the arch, seem to suggest an infinite resonance. It was only natural, in view of their cultural background, that the two artists should have so much in common in their interests and approach. Raphael, as the younger man, undoubtedly looked to the more experienced Bramante for support and guidance. In Rome, as a matter of fact, he lived in a palace which Bramante had designed, and which he himself finished building. Above all, Raphael took Bramante not only as a model for the space composition and setting of his paintings, but as the fundamental point of departure for all his work as an architect.

For Raphael, as a complete man of the Renaissance, aspiring to universal knowledge, was very soon attracted to the problems involved in designing churches and palaces. His plans for the church of Sant'Eligio degli Orefici, later built by Baldassare Peruzzi and restyled in the early seventeenth century by Flaminio Ponzio, were drawn up just after 1509, at the very time when he was painting his frescoes in the Stanza della Segnatura, and they clearly owe much to Bramante, particularly to his designs for Santa Maria del Popolo. In 1512 Raphael was commissioned to build the Chigi stables by the same banker for whom he had painted his fresco of the

Raphael. The Mass of Bolsena, detail of the chair bearers ▶
and Swiss guards, 1512.
Stanza di Eliodoro, Vatican Palace.

Raphael. The Mass of Bolsena, detail of the upper part, 1512. Stanza di Eliodoro, Vatican Palace.

This initial sketch shows the very careful attention Raphael gave to the problem of light: he used it not only to create the atmosphere and setting of the action, but also to emphasize its significance. In the center and on each side, it varies in its intensity, throws the figures into relief, and heightens the drama of the scene. Each episode is given the lighting best suited to it, conveying the sense of awe, terror, and divine power appropriate to the subject. Yet, by fusing together the light vibrations and adjusting them to each other, Raphael arrives at a wholly classical synthesis of time, place, and action.

Raphael. Preparatory Study for St Peter Delivered from Prison by the Angel, 1513. Print Room, Uffizi, Florence.

Triumph of Galatea in the Farnesina, Chigi's fine villa on the west bank of the Tiber designed by Baldassare Peruzzi. With this experience behind him, and having assimilated the architectural principles put into practice by Bramante, which in themselves were wholly congenial to him, Raphael felt able to accept the pope's offer to succeed his friend as chief architect in charge of the work on the new church of St Peter's after Bramante's death in 1514. He accepted this heavy task tranquilly and modestly, sharing the responsibility at first with Fra Giocondo, "a learned and venerable friar over eighty years old," as he wrote on the first of July 1514 to his uncle Simone di Battista di Ciarla in Urbino, whom the pope had given him as an associate "so that I may learn from him the secrets of architecture and make myself perfect in this art."

Raphael went on working on his frescoes in the Stanze of the Vatican until 1517. He was assisted by many pupils and collaborators, whose share in the work steadily increased: Giulio Romano, Giovanni Francesco Penni, Raffaellino del Colle, Perino del Vaga, Giovanni da Udine, and others. His Vatican frescoes were so great and immediate a success that Raphael at once became a celebrity, and orders for pictures poured in from all sides. To cope with them he was forced to employ assistants. In the Stanza di Eliodoro however, begun in the latter half of 1511 and completed in 1514 (after the death of Julius II, which occurred in February 1513), Raphael's guiding hand, and not only his general conception, is still paramount. Here again he treated a theme imposed on him by the pope, but a theme which this time bore no reference to the spiritual powers of religion and the Church. The frescoes in the Stanza di Eliodoro have a more practical purpose: their message, in keeping with the character and aspirations of Julius II, is an explicitly political one. The presiding theme is divine intervention in defense of the Church, Rome, and the papacy. And that intervention is shown taking place with a certain violence, as if giving stern warning to any who might be tempted to offend against these august institutions. Here again the aim behind the paintings seems to be a *renovatio Romae*, a restoration of papal power, such as Julius II had attempted to carry out by ruthless political means in the eventful decade of his pontificate.

Taking them in chronological order, the frescoes in the Stanza di Eliodoro represent the *Expulsion of Heliodorus from the Temple*, the *Mass of Bolsena*, the *Angel Delivering St Peter from Prison*, and the *Meeting of Attila and Leo the Great*. The Biblical episodes on the ceiling are not the work of Raphael himself. The scene showing the robber general Heliodorus driven from the temple (illustrating an incident described in the Second Book of Maccabees) no doubt alludes to the energetic policy of Julius II in his struggle to regain papal territories held by usurpers; this interpretation is confirmed by the presence in the scene of the pope himself, seated aloft in his ceremonial chair on the left side of the fresco. The *Mass of Bolsena* illustrates the miracle of the Host which took place in 1263 at Bolsena, near Orvieto, when an unbelieving priest was amazed to see the blood of Christ ooze from the sacramental wafer; here again Pope Julius is portrayed, kneeling on the right. The *Angel Delivering St Peter from Prison* symbolizes the divine protection accorded to the founder of the Church. The *Meeting of Attila and Leo the Great* has an even more explicit symbolism, with the figures of St Peter and St Paul, swords in hand, hovering over the pope as guarantors of his

Raphael. Heliodorus Driven from the Temple, 1511-1512. Stanza di Eliodoro, Vatican Palace.

The robber general Heliodorus driven from the Temple: the subject, taken from the second Book of Maccabees in the Apocrypha, alludes to Julius II's resolute policy of reconquering the territories usurped from the Church. Though the theme comes from ancient history, Raphael brings it up to date by using a Renaissance setting and inserting contemporary figures. On the left sits Julius II, while his two chair bearers may be portraits of Giulio Romano and Marcantonio Raimondi, the famous engraver whose prints did so much to popularize Raphael's paintings. The handling of this historical scene differs from that of the large compositions in the Stanza della Segnatura: it shows a new emphasis on movement and dramatic effect. There is a significant resemblance between the horse trampling Heliodorus and Leonardo's studies for the equestrian monument of the tomb of Gian Giacomo Trivulzio.

Michelangelo (1475-1564). Ceiling Fresco in the Sistine Chapel, detail: The Flood, 1508-1512.

The expressive power of Michelangelo fascinated Raphael and decisively influenced him. He was deeply impressed by so gigantic an undertaking as the decoration of the Sistine ceiling: it could not but leave its mark on so sensitive an artist as Raphael. Continually drawing comparisons and profiting by them, he studied Michelangelo's work closely and showed a profound understanding of his conception and his technical means.

◄ *Raphael and his Pupils. The Burning of the Borgo, detail of the left side, 1514. Stanza dell'Incendio, Vatican Palace.*

power; the pope portrayed here has the features, not of Julius II, who had died in February 1513, but of his successor Leo X. The meeting of Leo the Great with Attila and his hordes had taken place on the river Mincio in North Italy, in the year 452; but Raphael gives the scene a Roman setting in which the Colosseum and several other monuments can be recognized.

All the scenes in the Stanza di Eliodoro again have a complex spatial setting, and, again, Raphael redeems the symbolism of the themes by making himself a mediator between past and present, by expressing with the utmost clarity the continuity of a tradition whose relevance to his own times, and to his own actions, he was fully aware of. Thus there is no sense of indifference in his attitude toward the themes, which in his hands are interpreted, adapted, and made contemporary. In the same way, in his glorification of the papacy and its spiritual and temporal power, his faith never wavers, and indeed his very genuine piety colors his interpretation of events. Raphael was probably a less fervent believer than Michelangelo, his great antagonist in the Sistine Chapel; certainly his faith was less troubled, less introspective, closer to that of the common people, and more obedient to established authority. But it would be a mistake to regard him as an uncommitted painter, a "blithe spirit" enamored of a pagan myth of unruffled felicity and freedom, concerned only to restore an antique order of beauty outside time and history. With Raphael, the studied dignity of the form represents the dignity of the idea, from which it is inseparable, in accordance with the Neo-Platonic conception of form as figuring forth the harmony of the universe, the divine imprint. In these years moreover, especially during the pontificate of Leo X,

who favored a revival of the antique style of decoration, dignity of form answered to the religious ideals of the Church of Rome, and in a sense anticipated the ideals of decorum and dignity, didactic in intent, of Counter Reformation art. Julius II and Leo X could never have applied to Michelangelo for any such art as this; they turned to Raphael for it and from him they obtained it.

In the Stanza di Eliodoro Raphael seems to move with greater ease and sureness; witness the majestic grouping and spacing of figures, the resonance of the colors, the surge and flow of movement. Again he shows how profitably he had studied Leonardo, who is known to have been in Rome in 1513; Leonardo's influence tells particularly in the movement of bodies and the intensity of the backgrounds. On the other hand, the plastic density of the figures betrays his renewed interest in Michelangelo. The Sistine ceiling had been completed in 1512, but a large part of the

Raphael. St Cecilia, 1514. ▶

The traditional type of altarpiece is here transformed, both in the arrangement of the composition and in the expression of the figures. Raphael thus created a new prototype which, for over two centuries to come, was used by all artists for their religious paintings.

Barely ten years had passed since his earliest known pictures imbued with the sense of fairy-like enchantment that Perugino, his master, gave his compositions. Now he expresses his religious convictions with sovereign ease in figures that seem very earthly and appeal at once to the spectator, who may well be dazzled by the dignity of the form, the psychological aptness of the expression, and the lucid harmony of the composition as a whole.

According to Vasari, the musical instruments at the feet of St Cecilia were painted by Giovanni da Udine.

Pinacoteca, Bologna.

Raphael. Portrait of a Cardinal, 1510-1511. Prado, Madrid.

◄ *Raphael. Portrait of Pope Leo X with Cardinals Giulio de' Medici and Luigi de' Rossi, about 1518. Uffizi, Florence.*

frescoes could be seen by August of the previous year. Vasari tells how, when Michelangelo was absent from Rome, "Bramante, having the key of the Sistine Chapel, showed it to his friend Raphael, so that he might learn Michelangelo's methods. And this was the reason why Raphael repainted the prophet Isaiah, which he had already finished in the church of Sant'Agostino; having seen Michelangelo's frescoes, he greatly improved and elevated his manner in this work, and gave it more majesty."

It must be remembered that Vasari had an unbounded admiration for Michelangelo, who in his eyes represented the highest point reached in the progress of painting; and he tended to give Michelangelo credit for anything achieved by other artists of the day. True enough, the prophet Isaiah in the church of Sant'Agostino, which Raphael painted in 1511-1512 (so there was no necessity for a clandestine visit to the Sistine Chapel), is wholly Michelangelesque. But the influence of Michelangelo, of his grand and majestic manner, had already appeared in the Stanza della Segnatura, particularly in the figure of Heraclitus, the last personage he added to the *School of Athens*. It appears too, better assimilated and more generalized, in the Stanza di Eliodoro, and is even more pronounced in the dynamic sweep of the action-packed scenes in the next room, the Stanza dell'Incendio. It is difficult to pin that influence down to specific elements, so thoroughly is it worked over and absorbed into the general texture of Raphael's style, giving it a new richness and flexibility.

The frescoes in the Stanza di Eliodoro show a new interest in color, so strong here as to become the determinant factor in the space construction of the *Mass of Bolsena* and the *Angel Delivering St Peter*

from Prison. It is generally assumed that Raphael must have owed this new interest in color to contacts with the Venetians, with Lorenzo Lotto and, above all, Sebastiano del Piombo. It has even been supposed that Lotto himself may have painted the group of Swiss guards and chair bearers kneeling on the right, beneath the pope.

That Raphael, so eager a student of everything concerned with painting, was familiar with the Venetian masters and the refinements of Venetian color, is undeniable. "He came from Urbino and from circles where contacts with Venice, and with Ferrara and Mantua, were continuous and profound," as the Italian scholar Anna Maria Brizio has observed in a recent article. "Only this fact can explain the constant pictorial quality of his style, the softness of his modeling, the links between figure and landscape, and the harmony which subdues the vivacity of the local colors to the effect of the whole." By "pictorial" is meant the feeling for form and mass rendered in terms of color rather than line. It is precisely this pictorial character of Raphael's art which, whatever it may owe to the Venetians (and in any case he turns it into something quite unVenetian), modifies the monumental plasticity of Michelangelo, tones it down and renders it less heroic—gives it, in a word, a more popular appeal.

Raphael adjusts his colors to a harmonic space of carefully measured proportions: in effect, the colors bring out and emphasize the harmony of those proportions. In the *Angel Delivering St Peter* it is the

Raphael. Portrait of a Lady with a Veil ("Donna Velata"). ▶
about 1516.
Pitti Palace, Florence.

play of light that marks off the phases of the action and underscores its import. This important picture shows quite clearly in what direction the main line of Raphael's development lies: he did indeed look closely at the Venetians, but that line starts out from Piero della Francesca (is there not an obvious parallel between this picture and Piero's famous night scene at Arezzo, the *Dream of Constantine*?) and proceeds by way of Leonardo.

The Vatican Stanze, then, reveal a new sensitivity to color, a new ardor for light, but light contained and controlled, never encroaching on form, never blurring the outlines of figures and objects. This rich and luminous coloring appears in other works of these same years, in both sacred and secular paintings: the *Foligno Madonna*, the masterpiece of 1511-1512; the portrait of *Baldassare Castiglione* of 1514-1515; the portrait of about 1516 representing a lady with a veil, known as the *Donna Velata*, with its mellow golden tones; the portrait of *Leo X with Cardinals Giulio de' Medici and Luigi de' Rossi*—to mention only a few outstanding examples.

In each picture, color is put to a different purpose, always in accordance with Raphael's personal vision but varying with the end he has in view. Now he uses it to emphasize the aristocratic bearing of his sitter, as in the *Portrait of a Cardinal* in the Prado, of 1510-1511; now to recreate the pagan myth of Galatea, in the Farnesina fresco of 1511. Color, in the Prado portrait, in the shape of a bold counterpoint of reds varying with the varied play of light, is made the vehicle of a searching psychological characterization. With Raphael, color is often a mental construction, treated with the same dignity with which he treats form, and built up around an intellectual concept, not on a sensual impulse or even a naturalistic basis.

So it is that his color varies endlessly, shading off into a subdued blend of muted tones in the *Portrait of Castiglione*; condensing under intense lighting on the bodies and draperies of the figures in the *Triumph of Galatea*; setting off vivid whites against light blues and deep reds and violets in the *Mass of Bolsena*, thus emphasizing the assured authority of Pope Julius shown kneeling by the altar; rising into an abstract symphony of rich-hued reds in the *Portrait of Leo X*, suggestive of the canniness and worldly wisdom of the Medici pope.

Raphael used color as an instrument which he continually refined upon and perfected as time passed and he gained in experience and knowledge. But his sense of color was not an acquired faculty. He was a born colorist, as is proved by such youthful masterpieces as the *Knight's Dream* and the *Three Graces*, and by the sunny coloring, so fresh and artless, of the early *Marriage of the Virgin*.

The frescoes in the Stanza dell'Incendio, begun in 1514 and finished in July 1517, are inferior in quality to those in the Stanza della Segnatura and the Stanza di Eliodoro. Apart from the general design, Raphael himself took very little share in the work. His hand can be detected only in the face of the woman holding two vessels on the right side of the *Burning of the Borgo* (the scene which gives its name to the room), and perhaps too in the portraits of Leo X and several cardinals in the *Battle of Ostia*. All the rest is thought to be the work of Giulio Romano (who must have painted the large central figure in the *Burning of the Borgo*), Giovanni Francesco Penni and Raffaellino del Colle. The ceiling paintings previously executed by Perugino were left intact by Raphael, "in tribute to his memory, out of the affection Raphael bore him," writes Vasari.

The themes illustrated in the Stanza dell'Incendio were probably suggested by Baldassare Castiglione, for in a letter written to him in 1514 Raphael says that he has made "designs in several manners on subjects proposed by Your Lordship." This room, decorated in honor of Leo X, illustrates events in church history in which earlier popes by the name of Leo had played a signal part. In the *Burning of the Borgo*, Leo IV, with a sign of the cross, extinguishes the fire that ravaged this quarter of Rome, in the vicinity of the Vatican, in the year 847. The *Battle of Ostia* commemorates the victory of Leo IV over the Saracens in 849. In both scenes the pope has been given the features of Leo X. The other two frescoes, the *Crowning of Charlemagne* and the *Justification*, refer to events in the pontificate of Leo III.

While the execution of these frescoes is ponderous and uninspired, the general design and the grouping of figures again reveal Raphael's consummate skill in the organization of space. The Incendio frescoes also show a new cultural orientation and a new interest in form.

As he extended his activities to other fields and came to play a more and more important part in the cultural life of early sixteenth-century Rome, Raphael undoubtedly felt himself to be the most natural and best qualified interpreter of the civilization of his day. He had already made his name as an architect with his work in Sant'Eligio degli Orefici, the Chigi stables, and the Chigi chapel in Santa Maria del Popolo—this in the very years when he was painting the Vatican frescoes, and before he had succeeded Bramante as architect in charge of building operations on the new St Peter's.

The fact is that Raphael owed his unequalled gift for space composition, exemplified in the Vatican frescoes, to an intuitive understanding of architectural principles and to a profound culture that enabled him to borrow forms and imagery wherever he found them and integrate them perfectly into his paintings.

His growing interest in architecture—a natural outcome of the conception, so typical of the Renaissance, of the artist as a universal creator—led him on to a deeper appreciation of classical culture, just as it had led Bramante to make a close study of the structural principles of ancient buildings. In this, Raphael was acting wholly in the spirit of that *latinitas*, that love of Latin antiquity, which inspired the humanistic program of Leo X. In the letter of 1514 addressed to his Uncle Simone, Raphael wrote: "As for my being in Rome, I cannot well be elsewhere at any time, for the sake of the work going forward on St Peter's, because I have taken the place of Bramante. But what more excellent place is there in the world than Rome?"

PAGE 106: *Raphael. Dome of the Church of Sant'Eligio degli Orefici, Rome, after 1509.* ▶

PAGE 107: *Donato Bramante (1444-1514). The Small Temple or Tempietto of San Pietro in Montorio, Rome, about 1502.* ▶

At the beginning of the sixteenth century Bramante moved from Milan to Rome, where he worked actively as both architect and painter. About 1502 he was commissioned by the king and queen of Spain to build the small temple (Tempietto) of San Pietro in Montorio, on the spot where the tomb of the apostle Peter was thought to be. This admirably harmonious structure, translating the classical spirit into modern terms, served as an example for all the artists in Rome; for Raphael himself it was a fundamental lesson in architectural design.

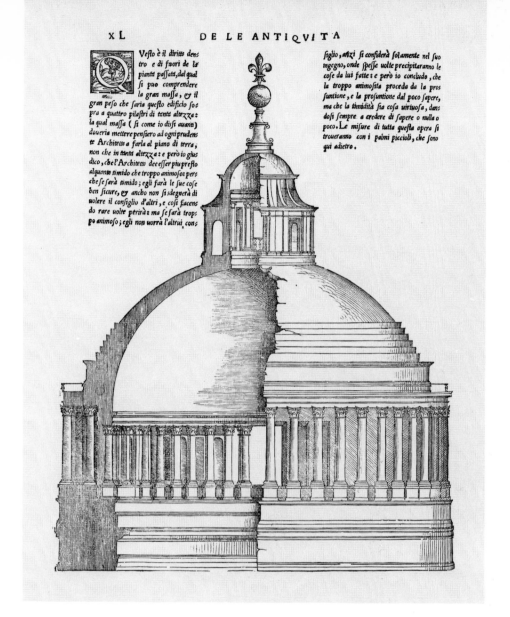

Vesto è il diritto dentro e di fuori de la pianta passata, dal qual si può comprendere la gran massa, & il gran peso che saria questo edificio sopra a quattro pilastri di tanta altezza: la qual massa (si come io dissi auanti) doueria mettere pensiero ad ogni prudente Architetto a farla al piano di terra, non che in tanta altezza: e però io gius dico, che l'Architetto dee esser più presto alquanto timido che troppo animoso: perche se sarà timido; egli farà le sue cose ben sicure, & ancho non si sdegnerà di uolere il consiglio d'altri, e così facendo rare uolte perirà: ma se sarà troppo animoso; egli non uorrà l'altrui con

siglio, anzi si confiderà solamente nel suo ingegno, onde spesse uolte precipitaranno le cose da lui fatte: e però io concludo, che la troppo animosità proceda da la presuntione, e la presuntione dal poco sapere, ma che la timidità sia cosa uirtuosa, dandosi sempre a credere di sapere o nulla o poco. Le misure di tutta questa opera si trouaranno con i palmi piccioli, che sono qui adietro.

Sebastiano Serlio (1475-1554). Plan and Section of the Dome designed by Bramante for St Peter's. Engraving from "Il Terzo Libro di Sebastiano Serlio...", Venice 1540.

◀ *Raphael. Interior of the Chigi Chapel in the Church of Santa Maria del Popolo, Rome, 1513-1516.*

Raphael. Study of God the Father for the Dome of the Chigi Chapel, about 1516. Drawing. Ashmolean Museum, Oxford.

◄ *Raphael. Study for an Angel in the Dome of the Chigi Chapel, about 1516. Drawing. Ashmolean Museum, Oxford.*

The references to classical antiquity, both to its literature and its architecture, are more evident in the Stanza dell'Incendio than in the earlier frescoes. The political ideal of the earlier work, inspired by Julius II, gives way to an archaeological program inspired by Leo X and his ideals of a *renovatio Romae*, a remaking of Rome. The scene of the *Burning of the Borgo*, with its foreshortened view of the façade of old St Peter's erected by Constantine, is meant to evoke the burning of Troy. The figures in the left foreground represent Aeneas, with his father Anchises on his back and his small son beside him, fleeing from the ruined city. Here, Raphael is alluding to the mythical origins of Rome, as described by Virgil, and emphasizing the historical continuity of the city's existence. Recognizable in the architectural setting of the scene are several buildings of ancient Rome such as the Temple of Mars Ultor and the Temple of Saturn. All this is strictly in keeping with the ideas of the pope —no longer the warlike Julius II, but the refined and cultivated son of Lorenzo the Magnificent. Thus Raphael too, like the humanist scholars of his time, turned back to the sources of Renaissance culture, to

◄ *Raphael. The Vision of Ezekiel, after 1516.*

Turning to account his experience as an architect, Raphael took to compositions marked by bold foreshortenings, like this small painting and also the preparatory studies for the dome of the Chigi Chapel.
The highly complex perspective gives rise to a picture space in which the figures seem to be projected backwards: the effect is not unlike that of stage scenery. And in fact Raphael designed some sets, notably for a performance of Ariosto's play I Suppositi *staged in the house of Monsignor Cibo in March 1519.*
Pitti Palace, Florence.

the surviving remains of classical antiquity. As he knew no Latin himself, he had his friend Fabio Calvo make for him an Italian translation of Vitruvius' treatise on architecture. In a letter to Calvo, dated August 15, 1514, he discusses certain passages and, for the interpretation of several terms, invokes the authority of Fra Giocondo, who had also made a translation of Vitruvius, dedicated to Julius II and published in Venice in 1511.

As Raphael grew older and more experienced, he showed an ever deeper interest in the monuments of antiquity—"these beautiful old wrecks," as he called them in his letter to Calvo. Not because he hoped to find in them a repertory of images worth taking over and copying; this would only have led him into a sham classicism. What he was looking for was the underlying significance and historical scope of ancient architecture. Like his friend Bramante, he made no attempt to imitate it. He turned to it as a means of testing not only the principles but even the techniques of his own work. His attitude to classical culture was very much the same as that of the humanist writers and poets with whom he had become friendly. One of them, Pietro Bembo, in a letter of April 3, 1516, to Cardinal Bibbiena, tells of an excursion planned for the next day, when he and his friends Beazzano, Navagero, Castiglione, and Raphael were going out to Tivoli (the ancient Tibur) to see "the old and the new, and whatever fine sights there may be in those parts."

Just a year before, on April 27, 1515, the pope had put Raphael in charge of the Vatican collection of stones bearing Latin inscriptions. In 1517 he appointed him curator of all the antiquities preserved in the Vatican. It would appear, from various accounts, that as such he was responsible for drawing up an

archaeological map of Rome. There still exists a long letter connected with this project, describing the condition of Rome at that time and the survey of its antiquities then being made. Judging by the style, the letter must have been written by Castiglione, but the matter contained in it is thought to have been supplied either by Raphael or by Bramante. A good case can be made for regarding this letter as Raphael's, addressed by him about 1519 to Pope Leo X.

It is a significant document, revealing in the man responsible for it an almost scientific interest in the monuments which he has studied, measured, classified, and appraised both for their artistic and their technical qualities. It is important too as testifying to the knowledge and judgment in cultural matters which Raphael—assuming the letter is Raphael's—had acquired in the years spent in Rome. "Having given much study to these antiquities," he writes, "and having taken no little pains to examine them in detail and measure them carefully, and having read the right authors unceasingly and compared the monuments with the texts, I think I have obtained some knowledge of this ancient architecture. On one account this has given me great pleasure, from all I have learned of so excellent a thing. But it is painful to behold almost the corpse, so miserably rent, of this beloved and noble city, once the queen of the world."

◀ *Andrea Palladio (1508-1580). Drawing of the Caprini Palace in Rome, designed by Bramante, bought and finished by Raphael.*
Royal Institute of British Architects, London.

◀ *Parmigianino (1503-1540). Drawing of the Aquila Palace in Rome, designed by Raphael.*
Print Room, Uffizi, Florence.

Further on, another passage in this letter affirms the cultural and technical unity of the different arts —those, that is, which the men of the Renaissance called the "arts of design." "Just as it is advisable for the painter to have some knowledge of architecture if he is to give his ornaments the right measurements and proportions, so must the architect have a knowledge of perspective, for by this means he may better imagine the edifice furnished with its ornaments."

The funerary chapel for the banker Agostino Chigi, which Raphael designed about 1513 in the church of Santa Maria del Popolo, was already a wholly successful attempt to put into actual practice this ideal conception of the unity of the arts. In this chapel Raphael acted at the same time as painter, sculptor, and architect. He not only provided the master plan of the chapel, made a model for the statue of Jonah riding the whale, which was then carved in marble by Lorenzetto, and drew the cartoons from which the dome mosaics were executed in 1516 by the Venetian Luigi Pace; he also saw to it that every part of the chapel was closely related to the other parts, so that it formed a unified whole. A *tour de force* in its perspective effects, the Chigi Chapel is unsurpassed in the boldness and skill of its design. Despite some Baroque additions, the architectural arrangement still retains its admirable clarity. The central plan may have been inspired by that of the Pantheon. Intended as the expression of an ideal place, its space rises up with a soaring movement reminiscent of Bramante, who only shortly before this had designed the dome of St Peter's. The lines of force of this mobile, enveloping space are not broken but emphasized by the movement of the Jonah statue. And its upward thrust is not arrested

Baldassare Peruzzi (1481-1536). The Farnesina, Rome.

Designed by Peruzzi, the Villa Chigi was built for the rich banker Agostino Chigi and decorated with paintings by Raphael, Sodoma, Giulio Romano, Sebastiano del Piombo, and Peruzzi himself. Sold about 1580 to Cardinal Alessandro Farnese, the villa has since been known as the Farnesina. After painting the Galatea in 1511, Raphael supervised the decoration of the loggia, about 1516-1517, with scenes from the myth of Cupid and Psyche.

Raphael. The Triumph of Galatea, 1511. Fresco in the Farnesina, Rome. ▶

Raphael. The Three Graces, 1516. Study for the right side of the Nuptial Banquet on Olympus *decorating the Loggia of Psyche in the Farnesina, Rome. Royal Library, Windsor Castle.*

◄ *Raphael. Psyche Bringing to Venus the Jar Containing the Ointment of Beauty, 1516. Study for the Loggia of Psyche in the Farnesina, Rome. Cabinet des Dessins, Louvre, Paris.*

Plan of the Villa Madama in Rome. Engraving from "Choix des plus célèbres maisons de plaisance de Rome et de ses environs.
Mesurées et dessinées par Charles Percier et P. F. L. Fontaine," Paris 1808.

by the dome, but continues to move and expand in the concentric circles of the mosaic decoration, rising into the uppermost circle where God the Father is represented, not as the motionless godhead of Aristotle's philosophy, but as the motive force of the Neo-Platonists, suggesting the infinite universe. Here, as in the Stanza della Segnatura and the Stanza di Eliodoro, Raphael is seen at his greatest, the grand master of an art that transcends the accepted limits of space, going well beyond the canons fixed by Bramante and creating a spatial conception unexampled in Renaissance art.

As an architect, Raphael did an astonishing amount of work, considering how short his life was and how brief the period of his maturity. After succeeding Bramante as chief architect of St Peter's, he changed the central plan devised by the latter into a cruciform plan; in this he was undoubtedly acting in accordance with the wishes of the new pope. But Leo X did not show as much interest in St Peter's as Julius II, and the work progressed so slowly that Raphael died before he had had time to leave his impress on the new basilica.

According to Vasari, Raphael "designed the villa in the pope's vineyard and several houses in the Borgo quarter, in particular the palace of Messer Giovan Battista dell'Aquila, which was a very fine piece of work. He also designed a palace for the bishop of Troia, who had it built in Florence in the Via di San Gallo." The Aquila Palace was pulled down in the seventeenth century to make way for Bernini's colonnade in front of St Peter's; all that now remains is a drawing of it attributed to Parmigianino. The Pandolfini Palace, built for the bishop of Troia (whose name was Pandolfini), still exists, but its attribution to Raphael is questioned by present-day scholars. The villa erected in the papal vineyard, known as the Villa Madama (after it became the property of Margaret of Austria, daughter of the Emperor Charles V), was probably begun after 1516. It is a landmark in the development of Italian architecture. The unity between structure and decoration is perfect, even though the latter was carried out by his pupils. A system of proportions is created not only in terms of mass but in terms of light, and the building is admirably adapted to the lie of the land and the natural surroundings. Raphael here struck out on his own, going far beyond the lessons of Bramante, and the originality of this elegant villa had a direct influence on the great architects who came after him in Italy, notably on Giulio Romano, who worked under Raphael for years, and later Palladio.

Raphael succeeded Bramante as chief architect not only of St Peter's but also of the Vatican palaces, where he took charge of the construction and decoration of the open galleries known as the Loggie—"begun by Bramante but unfinished at his death, and then continued on a new plan by Raphael" (Vasari). This complex sequence of decorations, not to be completed until the early months of 1519, was executed by a team of artists working under the supervision of the master. "Raphael," writes Vasari, "designed the stucco ornaments and the pictures. He placed Giovanni da Udine in charge of the stuccoes and grotesques, and Giulio Romano in charge of the figure paintings, although the latter did little of the work. And so Giovanni Francesco Penni, Bologna (Tommaso Vincidor), Perino del Vaga, Pellegrino da Modena, Vincenzo da San Gimignano and Polidoro da Caravaggio, with many other painters, did the pictures and figures, and such other paintings as the work called for."

Every member of Raphael's workshop was called into action and the decorations were executed in a genuine spirit of teamwork. His pupils were not left to carry out a plan drawn up for them in advance, as was usually the case in such work. From the start it was a collective undertaking, all the artists cooperating under Raphael's guidance. Serenely confident in himself and in the principles and standards which he had transmitted to his pupils, Raphael gave them a free hand not only in the execution but in the planning of the work, which was discussed and decided on jointly. He took it for granted that he and they would be of one mind. Vasari says of him: "He was always surrounded by countless pupils, helping and instructing them with an affection more like that of a man for his own sons than for his associates."

For Raphael had created a method, a style, a repertory of images, a theory and practice of painting, which shaped and colored all the work that came out of his studio. The work of all his assistants became in effect the projection of his own personality and bore the stamp of his authority. After his death, his studio assistants carried his message and lesson all over Italy, diffusing it to an extent that had no precedent.

Although they have suffered from exposure to the weather (the open galleries were not glassed in until the nineteenth century), the Loggie frescoes have an unimpaired charm and beauty. Nothing could be less like Michelangelo than these delightful pictures, which were certainly very much to the taste of the pope and the Roman aristocracy. Complex, nevertheless, in the variety of their techniques and the range of their themes, they cover the ceiling, walls, arches and pillars. In the thirteen bays of the vaulted ceiling are Biblical scenes, from the Old Testament in the first twelve, from the New Testament in the thirteenth. The stucco reliefs represent mythological themes, ancient and modern sculptures (Donatello's *St George*, for example), and even contemporary scenes (one of them shows Raphael's pupils at work).

The Loggie decorations are lively and cheerful, graceful and refined, yet wholly popular in their appeal. If compared with the mighty energy and ringing chords of Michelangelo's Sistine ceiling, they seem almost as sprightly and skipping as a scherzo. No wonder that for centuries the Loggie frescoes have been popularly known as "Raphael's Bible." Anything dramatic or disturbing in the sacred themes illustrated is conjured away by the grace and charm of the forms, by the bright, fresh colors. Each scene has its place in an ordered sequence whose progression is marked by architectural elements bathed in light. From this happy, smiling world, doubt and anxiety have been banished.

Raphael had also designed the decorations of another loggia, that of the Farnesina; the execution he left to his pupils, who finished it in 1517. The owner of this villa on the west bank of the Tiber was the banker Agostino Chigi, who was one of the artist's greatest admirers. For him, in 1511, Raphael had painted the *Triumph of Galatea*, also in the Farnesina; for him he had built the chapel in Santa Maria del

◄ *Baldassare Peruzzi (1481-1536). Perspective Painting, about 1515. Farnesina, Rome.*

Baldassare Peruzzi not only designed and built the Farnesina, but also painted the ceiling decorations in the Hall of the Galatea, the Hall of the Frieze, and the Hall of the Perspectives. This artist—who also painted part of the ceiling frescoes in the Vatican Stanze—spent about ten years working on the sumptuous villa of Agostino Chigi.

Popolo and painted some frescoes, about 1514, in another chapel in Santa Maria della Pace. The design of the Farnesina itself has been attributed to Raphael. Actually the villa was begun about 1505 by Baldassare Peruzzi, who also decorated several of the rooms with frescoes, among them a perspective view of a Roman landscape, painted with complete illusionism. One of the lordliest palaces in Rome, the Farnesina—or Villa Chigi, as it was then called—was in every way worthy of its wealthy owner and the regal banquets he was fond of giving there. It was the ideal setting for the play of Raphael's fancy.

The loggia he was to decorate stood on the ground floor; at that time it opened on the garden of the villa. The theme of the frescoes was drawn from classical literature: they illustrate the story of Psyche as told by Apuleius in *The Golden Ass*. Several of Raphael's preliminary sketches still exist. The frescoes themselves, admirably adapted to their architectural setting, were painted by his pupils, Giulio Romano, Penni, and several others. Here again the theme and treatment of the decorations must have answered perfectly to the taste of the cultivated circles in which Raphael moved in Rome.

On the strength of a tradition that goes back to Vasari, it has generally been assumed that toward the end of his life Raphael overstrained his powers and impaired his natural style out of a desire to emulate the grandiose manner of Michelangelo. Raphael had always been receptive to outside influences. From the beginning his style had been shaped and reshaped by successive contacts and encounters, and he profited to the full by the lessons to be learned from Piero della Francesca and Perugino, Bramante and Michelangelo. But he had always shown a wonderful power of assimilating and synthesizing whatever he took from others. All that he took, he combined into a perfected style, inimitably his own.

Certainly the example of Michelangelo, the heroic energy of his figures, and his devotion to his art, impressed him and gave him food for thought. He may well have seen in Michelangelo an inspiring example of a moral commitment. But his own conception of the world, and of his art, was totally different, and the forms and colors in which he clothed his conceptions were his own. Think of the long series of his portraits and the ideal of aristocratic superiority of mind which they express, the sense of timeless permanence he imparts to these pictures of scholars and churchmen, women and popes, who are, nevertheless, such real, flesh-and-blood presences. All this is admirably realized in the late portrait of *La Fornarina*, datable to about 1518-1519, even though it is largely the work of Giulio Romano: it is a figure at once earthbound and aloof, carnal and timeless, a tantalizing synthesis of soft, warm color harmonies and precise, firmly moulded forms.

In his religious compositions, too, Raphael arrived at a satisfying equilibrium between grandiose, monumental forms, undoubtedly derived from Michelangelo, and a majestic space composition in which the norms of Renaissance perspective are boldly

Giulio Romano (1499-1546) and Raphael. Portrait of a ▶ *Woman, about 1518-1519.*

The woman represented in this portrait, and also in the portrait of the "Donna Velata," is La Fornarina (meaning, literally, "woman baker"). Her real name was Margherita Luti, she came from Siena, and she was in fact a baker's daughter. She became famous as Raphael's mistress and model during his Roman period.
Galleria Nazionale di Arte Antica, Rome.

transgressed—a procedure he had already experimented with, and carried even further, in the *Vision of Ezekiel*. Probably painted shortly after 1516, this small panel, with its bold foreshortening of the main figure, again conveys the suggestion of infinite space that had transfigured the vision of God the Father in the dome of the Chigi Chapel.

Although he was a respecter of tradition and took his stand on the values handed down to him, Raphael renewed and in some cases transformed them. Such masterpieces as the *Sistine Madonna* of 1513-1514 and the *St Cecilia*, ordered from him in 1514, departed from the traditional composition of the altarpiece and established a new type which lasted for centuries, down to the time of Ingres. Its novelty lay not only in the composition, in the compactness and rationality of the layout, but also in a psychological revaluation of the sacred figures and the role he assigned them as mediators between God and man. Vasari felt something of this when he recorded the Latin verses composed in homage to the *St Cecilia*: "Let others paint the face alone, reproducing it with colors. Of Cecilia, Raphael has shown both face and soul." The passions and feelings, the movements of the body and the mind are compounded into the coherent expression of a balanced personality. This harmony of the physical and spiritual informs not only the portraits and altar paintings but also the great decorative cycles, like the tapestry cartoons ordered for

◀ *Raphael and his Pupils. The Vatican Loggie, detail of the stucco decoration, 1517-1519.*

Raphael and his Pupils. Overall View of the Vatican ▶ *Loggie, 1517-1519.*

the Sistine Chapel by Leo X toward the end of 1514, and sent to Brussels to be woven in the workshop of Pieter van Aelst.

Raphael's last painting was the *Transfiguration*. This altarpiece was commissioned in 1517—in competition with Sebastiano del Piombo, who painted a *Raising of Lazarus*—by Cardinal Giulio de' Medici for the cathedral of Narbonne, in France, of which he was bishop. Raphael does not appear to have finished the picture himself. When he died it was placed at his bedside; three years later it was set up in the church of San Pietro in Montorio in Rome; it is now in the Vatican picture gallery. Raphael's dramatic and inventive powers are seen at their highest in the shifting lights and ascending rhythms that unite the agitated figures in the lower part to the serene vision of glory above. This work strikes a deeper chord than ever before. It is like a solemn warning of impending calamities—the knell of a world about to fall from grace and contend with stern realities. The *Transfiguration* is poignant proof of a deepened consciousness of the Christian message. The composition and the handling of forms seem to overleap the Mannerist period, which lay immediately ahead, and prefigure the Baroque style of the seventeenth century.

Raphael died in Rome on Good Friday, April 6, 1520, his thirty-seventh birthday. His death was felt by all like the death of a god, and the end of a myth. It was said that, just as the Temple of Solomon cracked at the death of Christ, the Vatican palace cracked when Raphael died. With his passing, Renaissance Rome lost its spokesman. "So many great ancients and so long an age went to the making of Rome; so many enemies and centuries went to destroy it. Now Raphael seeks and finds Rome in Rome: it is for a great man to seek, it is for God to find," wrote Celio Calcagnini of Raphael in a Latin epigram. His body was entombed in the Pantheon. "When this noble artist died," wrote Vasari, "painting would fain have died with him, for when he closed his eyes, she became almost blind."

Raphael. The Transfiguration, detail of the upper part, 1518-1520. Pinacoteca, Vatican City.

IN QUEST OF RAPHAEL IN ROME

BIBLIOGRAPHY

INDEX AND BIOGRAPHICAL NOTICES

LIST OF ILLUSTRATIONS

1. St Peter's and the Vatican

2. Villa Madama

3. Santa Maria del Popolo

4. The Farnesina

5. Santa Maria della Pace

6. Sant'Agostino

7. Sant'Eligio degli Orefici

Viale Giulio Cesare

P. Navona

Corso Vittorio Emanuele

A SHORT BIBLIOGRAPHY

From Ariosto to Goethe and Baudelaire, and from Poussin to Reynolds and Renoir, the great writers, poets and painters have all had something to say about Raphael. The number of works dealing with his life and art is very large, beginning in his lifetime with the writings of his contemporaries and with his first biographers in the sixteenth century, Paolo Giovio and Giorgio Vasari. Since that time, Raphael has been referred to, at length or in passing, in every book concerned with the history of painting. In this short bibliography we have listed some of the most informative and most easily accessible studies published since the nineteenth century, not only of the artist himself but of his background, his milieu, and various aspects of his art. We have chosen above all those works which we found most useful in the writing of this book.

L. PUNGILEONI, *Elogio storico di Raffaello Santi da Urbino*, Urbino 1829. — K. F. VON RUMOHR, *Über Raphael von Urbino und seine Verhältnisse zu den Zeitgenossen*, Berlin and Stettin 1831. — J. B. PASSAVANT, *Raphael von Urbino und sein Vater Giovanni Santi*, 2 vols., Leipzig 1839-1858. — J. BURCKHARDT, *Der Cicerone*, Basel 1855. — J. BURCKHARDT, *Geschichte der Renaissance in Italien*, Leipzig 1867. — H. GRIMM, *Das Leben Raphaels*, Berlin 1872. — G. B. CAVALCASELLE and J. A. CROWE, *Raphael, His Life and Works*, London 1882-1885. — H. VON GEYMÜLLER, *Raffaello Sanzio studiato come architetto*, Milan 1884. — E. MÜNTZ, *Raphaël, sa vie, son œuvre et son temps*, Paris 1886. — R. VISCHER, *Studien für Kunstgeschichte*, Stuttgart 1886. — D. GUOLI, *Documenti relativi a Raffaello di Urbino*, Archivio Storici dell'Arte, II, 1889, p. 250. — B. BERENSON, *The Central Italian Painters of the Renaissance*, London 1897. — H. WÖLFFLIN, *Renaissance und Barock*, Munich 1899. — O. FISCHEL, *Raphael*, in U. Thieme and F. Becker, *Künstler Lexicon* (with extensive bibliography up to 1935), Leipzig 1907-1950. — T. HOFFMANN, *Raphael in seiner Bedeutung als Architekt*, 4 vols., Leipzig 1908-1911. — A. ROSENBERG and G. GRONAU, *Raphael*, Stuttgart and Leipzig 1909. — J. VOGEL, *Bramante und Raphael*, Leipzig 1910. — O. FISCHEL, *Raphaels Zeichnungen*, I-VIII, Berlin 1913-1941. — A. VENTURI, *La lettera di Raffaello a Leone X sulla pianta di Roma antica*, in L'Arte, XXI, 1918. — A. VENTURI, *Raffaello*, Urbino 1920; new edition revised by Lionello Venturi, Milan 1952. — E. PANOFSKY, *Idea*, Leipzig 1924. — E. PANOFSKY, *Die Perspektive als symbolische Form*, Vorträge der Bibliothek Warburg, 1924-1925, 1927. — C. GAMBA, *Raphaël*, Paris 1926. — W. WAUSCHER, *Raffaello Santi da Urbino, His Life and Works*, London 1926. — F. HERMANIN, *La Farnesina*, Bergamo 1927. — L. VENTURI, *Il gusto dei primitivi*, Bologna 1929. — B. BERENSON, *Italian Painters of the Renaissance*, Oxford 1932. — V. GOLZIO, *Raffaello nei documenti, nelle testimonianze e nella letteratura del suo secolo*, Vatican City 1936. — L. VENTURI, *History of Art Criticism*, New York 1936. - D. GNOLI, *La Roma di Leone X*, Milan 1938. — E. GARIN, *Il Rinascimento italiano*, Florence 1941. — S. ORTOLANI, *Raffaello*, Bergamo 1942. — P. ROTONDI, *Il Palazzo ducale di Urbino nella formazione di Raffaello*, in *Studi Urbinati*, XV, 1942. — P. O. KRISTELLER, *Humanism and Scholasticism in the Italian Renaissance*, in *Byzantion*, XVII, 1944-1945, p. 346 ff. — D. REDIG DE CAMPOS, *Raffaello e Michelangelo*, Rome 1946. — G. J. HOOGEWERFF, *La Stanza della Segnatura*, in *Rendiconti della Pontificia Accademia*, XXIII, Rome 1947-1949. — R. WITTKOWER, *Architectural Principles in the Age of Humanism*, London 1949. — D. REDIG DE CAMPOS, *Le Stanze di Raffaello*, Florence 1950. — M. SALMI, *La "Renovatio Romae" e Firenze*, in *Rinascimento*, I, 1950, pp. 115-124. — P. FRANCASTEL, *Peinture et Société*, Lyons 1951. — G. J. HOOGEWERFF, *Leonardo e Raffaello*, in *Commentari*, III, 1952, pp. 173-183. — D. REDIG DE CAMPOS, *Dei ritratti di Antonio Tebaldeo e d'altri nel Parnaso di Raffaello*, in *Archivio della Società romana di Storia patria*, LXXV, 1952, pp. 51-58. — A. CHASTEL, *Marsil Ficin et l'Art*, Geneva 1954. — P. D'ANCONA, *Gli affreschi della Farnesina*, Milan 1955. — R. LONGHI, *Percorso di Raffaello giovine*, in *Paragone*, VI, 1955, pp. 8-23. — E. BATTISTI, *Il concetto d'imitazione nel Cinquecento da Raffaello a Michelangelo*, in *Commentari*, VII, 1956, pp. 86-104. — E. CAMESASCA, *Tutta la pittura di Raffaello*, 2 vols., Milan 1956. — E. CAMESASCA, *Tutti gli scritti di Raffaello*, Milan 1956. — O. H. FÖRSTER, *Bramante*, Vienna and Munich 1956. — L. VENTURI, *The Sixteenth Century, From Leonardo to El Greco*, Geneva 1956. — H. B. GUTMANN, *Zur Ikonologie der Fresken Raphaels in der Stanza della Segnatura*, in *Zeitschrift für Kunstgeschichte*, XXI, 1958, pp. 27-39. — W. SCHÖNE, *Raphael*, Berlin and Darmstadt 1958. — C. G. STRIDBECK, *Raphael Studies*, Stockholm 1958. — A. CHASTEL, *Art et Humanisme à Florence au temps de Laurent le Magnifique*, Paris 1959. — A. BERTINI, *La trasfigurazione e l'ultima evoluzione della pittura di Raffaello*, in *La Critica d'Arte*, VIII, 1961. — C. L. FROMMEL, *Die Farnesina und Peruzzi architektonisches Frühwerk*, Berlin 1961. — A. M. BRIZIO, *Raphael*, in *Encyclopedia of World Art*, Vol. XI, New York 1966. — *Raffaello*, introduction by Michele PRISCO, biographical and critical apparatus by Pierluigi DE VECCHI, Milan 1966.

AELST Pieter van (active 1497-1531) 128.

AGESANDER of Rhodes (1st century B.C.) 85.

ALBERTI Leon Battista (Genoa c. 1404-Rome 1472) 13, 16, 20/23, 27, 28, 36, 40, 41, 61, 89;
On Statuary 28.

The son of a Florentine exile, he received a thorough classical education. Worked in Rome from 1431, in Florence from 1434. Poet, scholar, theorist and architect, he was a great student of ancient art. He had a lofty conception of art and the artist's role, considering the highest aspirations of the human mind to be embodied in creative activity. He wrote on many subjects, including three famous treatises on painting, sculpture and architecture *(De Pictura, De Statua, De Re Aedificatoria)*. Especially active as an architect. For Sigismondo Malatesta he transformed the Tempio Malatestiano in Rimini. In Mantua he designed the churches of Sant'Andrea and San Sebastiano. In Florence he remodeled the façade of Santa Maria Novella and left his mark on civil architecture with the construction of the Rucellai Palace. The execution of his works, several of which remained incomplete, was usually left to his assistants.

ALBIZZINI family 40.

ALEXANDER VI Borgia, Pope (1492-1503) 67.

APULEIUS (2nd century A.D.), *The Golden Ass* 124.

ARIOSTO (1474-1533) 86, 113;
I Suppositi (1519) 113.

ARISTOTLE (384-322 B.C.) 7, 75, 76, 121.

ATHENODORUS of Rhodes (2nd century B.C.) 85.

BAGLIONI Atalanta 58, 59, 61;
Grifonetto, her son (d. 1500) 58, 61.

BARTOLOMEO DELLA GATTA (Florence 1448-c. 1503) 67.

His real name was Piero d'Antonio Dei. Son of a goldsmith, he entered, very young, the Camaldulensian monastery of the Angioli and in 1470 was transferred to Santa Maria in Gradi at Arezzo. He was influenced by Signorelli and Perugino and knew the paintings of Piero della Francesca. Perugino summoned him to Rome in 1481 to work in the Sistine Chapel. There he saw and admired Melozzo da Forlì. Decorated various Tuscan churches and monasteries and worked at Loreto. A man of many talents—musician, miniaturist, architect, organ-builder.

BARTOLOMEO DELLA PORTA Fra (Florence 1475-Pian di Mugnone 1517) 58.

His real name was Bartolomeo di Paolo del Fattorino. Painter and Dominican friar, trained in the Florentine workshop of Cosimo Rosselli, together with Piero di Cosimo and Mariotto Albertinelli. After a series of works in the Quattrocento manner, he followed in the footsteps of the great masters of the early Cinquecento, Leonardo and Michelangelo, cultivating an eclecticism which is a little ponderous and theatrical. His style, however, is stately and correct, and through him (among others) the innovations of Tuscan art spread to Venice, which he visited in 1508, being influenced in his turn by Venetian colorism. Among his most notable works are a *Last Judgment* (1499) for the hospital of Santa Maria Nuova in Florence (now in the Uffizi, Florence), an altarpiece with *God Appearing to St Catherine and St Margaret* (Lucca Museum), the *Marriage of St Catherine* (1511, Louvre) and a *Deposition* of 1511 (Pitti Palace, Florence).

BAUDELAIRE Charles (1821-1867) 7.

BEMBO Pietro (Venice 1470-Rome 1547) 86, 113.

Son of a Venetian patrician and ambassador, he was early familiarized with the leading humanist courts of Italy. Studied Greek under Constantine Lascaris in Sicily and philosophy at Padua University. Lived at the court of Urbino where he met Giovanni de' Medici who, when he became pope as Leo X, summoned Bembo to Rome. Though a great Latinist, he wrote an Italian dialogue on Platonic love, *Gli Asolani*, and in an essay *Della Volgar Lingua* he defended the use of Italian for literary purposes: he was an important influence on the shaping of modern Italian prose.

Berlin, Staatliche Museen 19.

BERNINI Gian Lorenzo (1598-1680) 121.

BERRUGUETE Pedro (Paredes de Nava, Castile c. 1450-Avila 1504) 14, 17.

Probably trained in the entourage of Fernando Gallego, he was strongly influenced by Flemish art before coming to Italy shortly before 1477, summoned to Urbino by Federico di Montefeltro. Together with Justus of Ghent, he painted a series of prophets and philosophers to decorate the library of the Ducal Palace. These 28 pictures of "Famous Men" are now divided between the Louvre and the Urbino museum. The Flemish element in his style is much stronger than the Italian, though he owed something to Melozzo da Forlì and much to Piero della Francesca, whose work he saw at Urbino. He was the father of the great sculptor Alonso Berruguete.

BIBBIENA (1470-1520) 113.

His real name was Bernardo Dovizi. Taken up when still very young by the Medici court in Florence, he was sent on diplomatic missions to Rome and Naples. When the Medici were driven out of Florence, he followed Cardinal Giovanni de' Medici (later Pope Leo X) to Rome as his private secretary. Lived at Urbino in the circle of Bembo, Castiglione, Elisabetta Gonzaga, Isabella d'Este and Giuliano de' Medici, and there he probably wrote his prose comedy *Calandria*, first presented at

Urbino in 1513 by Baldassare Castiglione. After the restoration of the Medici and the election of Leo X, he was appointed papal treasurer, protonotary, and count palatine (1513). That same year he was made a cardinal. His letters are of great interest and importance. Raphael was engaged to be married to one of his nieces; she died shortly before the artist himself.

BOCCACCIO (1313-1375) 14, 86.
Bologna, Pinacoteca 98, 99.
BORGIA Cesare (1475/6-1507) 13.

BRAMANTE Donato (1444-1514) 16, 22, 27, 36, 40, 67, 83, 86, 90, 94, 102, 105, 107, 109, 113, 115, 121, 124.

Born at Monte Asdrualdo near Urbino. Trained in Urbino as painter and architect. Went to Lombardy, working in Bergamo, then in Milan in the service of Ludovico il Moro. In Milan he designed the church of Santa Maria presso San Satiro and the adjoining baptistery, took part in the building of Pavia Cathedral, built the central part of Santa Maria delle Grazie in Milan, designed the façade of Santa Maria Nuova at Abbiategrasso (near Milan), and painted a series of frescoes in the Casa Panigarola, Milan (now in the Brera). Moving to Rome in 1499, he designed the Tempietto of San Pietro in Montorio, the cloister of Santa Maria della Pace, and the choir of Santa Maria del Popolo. Julius II set him to work in the Vatican, where he designed the new St Peter's and supervised its construction from 1506; by the time he died he had raised the four great piers and built the arches of the transept. His monumental conception of space, already clear in Milan, reached in Rome a classical perfection of balanced masses and stately harmony. To this effect contributed his preference for central plans: the Tempietto is circular and his design for St Peter's took the form of a Greek cross surmounted by a dome. But St Peter's was changed a good deal after his death, passing through various phases, until finally Michelangelo, when he was put in charge of building operations in 1547, reverted to the central plan of Bramante, and to his general conception.

BRAMANTINO (c. 1465-1536) 67.

His real name was Bartolomeo Suardi. A painter and architect whose background is obscure. Studied in Milan under Bramante (hence the name by which he is known) and in 1503 was working in Milan Cathedral. In 1508 he was at the Vatican, summoned perhaps by Bramante, and painted part of the ceiling in the Stanza della Segnatura. In 1511 he seems to have been in Naples, decorating San Domenico Maggiore (Carafa Chapel). His masterpiece is the Trivulzio Chapel (1519) in San Nazzaro, Milan. In 1525 he was appointed court painter and architect, and also chief military engineer, by Duke Francesco Maria Sforza of Milan. In his architectural designs he kept to Bramante's stately and classical conception of space. In his painting, he was influenced by the Milanese master Butinone, then by Leonardo and Bramante; his style took on a classical strain in Rome. Characteristic paintings, all in Milan, are an *Adoration of the Magi* (Ambrosiana), *Lucretia* (Sala-Busca Collection), and the *Crucifixion* (Brera).

BRIZIO Anna Maria 102.

BRUNELLESCHI Filippo (Florence 1379-1446) 36, 40.

Began as a goldsmith and sculptor, then devoted himself to architecture, of which he was the first great innovator of the 15th century. Took part (1402) in the competition for the bronze doors of the Florentine Baptistery (won by Ghiberti) with a panel representing the *Sacrifice of Isaac*: this, like his other sculptures (Crucifix of Santa Maria Novella), already shows the new vision of reality which he soon worked out in architecture in a scientific definition of space by means of perspective. Proved his ability as a technician by roofing Santa Maria del Fiore with a dome that needed no wooden armatures to hold it up. Among other buildings he designed in Florence, on a strictly classical plan, with structure and decoration in perfect harmony, are the Ospedale degli Innocenti, the church and sacristy of San Lorenzo, the church of Santo Spirito, also the Rotonda degli Angeli and the Palazzo Pitti. His scientific humanism and his application of the rules of perspective strongly influenced the painters and all the artists of the early Renaissance.

Budapest, Museum of Fine Arts 53.

Caen, Musée des Beaux-Arts 34, 40.

CALCAGNINI Celio (1479-1541) 128.

A cultivated humanist, he served on diplomatic missions for the Emperor Maximilian and Pope Julius II. Papal legate at the Este court, he also lectured on literature at Ferrara University. A friend of Erasmus of Rotterdam and Ariosto, he wrote on many subjects.

CALVO Fabio 113.

CASTIGLIONE Baldassare (1478-1529) 7, 13, 23, 26/28, 89, 104, 105, 113, 115;
The Book of the Courtier 13, 27, 89.

One of the outstanding scholars and writers of the 16th century, he came of a noble Lombard family established in Mantua. Employed by the Gonzagas, he traveled widely on diplomatic and political missions, notably to Rome and Urbino. Especially attracted by the latter town, he passed into the service of Guidobaldo di Montefeltro, for whom he traveled much in Italy and abroad as special envoy. Life at the court of Urbino inspired his masterpiece, *Il Libro del Cortegiano* (The Book of the Courtier), a vivid reflection of Renaissance life and the ideals of his time. He served as ambassador at the court of Julius II and was a close friend of Raphael, who painted his portrait (Louvre). Continued to frequent the papal court under Leo X and Clement VII, serving the latter on diplomatic missions in Spain, where he died.

A member of the same family as Baldassare, he joined the Knights of St John of Jerusalem (Knights of Malta) and became procurator-general of the order. In 1517 he received the commendam of the church of Santa Maria Maddalena at Faenza, and there he lived for the rest of his life. A cultivated humanist and connoisseur of the arts, he wrote a well-known didactic work, *Ricordi ovvero Ammaestramenti* (1546); it treats of the moral life and accomplishments of a gentleman, and contains some shrewd observations on the art of his time.

Trained in the Florentine workshops of the 1390's, when the art of Nanni di Banco and Lorenzo Ghiberti was in the ascendant. He gave a new direction to sculpture, which for him was an instrument of research into the spirit of man and his role in history. Particularly active in Florence, he worked for the Cathedral (Porta della Mandorla), Orsanmichele (St George), and the Campanile (Prophets). For Siena he executed *Herod's Feast* (1427), one of the first works in which he used the peculiar technique of *stiacciato* (flattened or half-flat relief) enabling him to achieve effects of spatial perspective similar to those of Brunelleschi. About 1432 he was in Rome. From 1433 to 1443 he worked chiefly in Florence (organ loft of the Cathedral, sacristy decorations in San Lorenzo, *Annunciation* in Santa Croce, etc.). From 1443 to 1452 he was in Padua working on the marble altar screen in the church of St Anthony and the equestrian statue of the Gattamelata, masterpieces of inspired realism. His last works, and some of his most expressive, were made after his return to Florence (*Mary Magdalen* for the Baptistery, two pulpits for San Lorenzo, *John the Baptist* for Siena Cathedral).

A modest painter employed in Giovanni Santi's workshop as an assistant in 1483. Became executor of his will and a member, along with Raphael, of the confraternity of the Blessed Sacrament in Urbino. He collaborated with Raphael on the altarpiece of St Nicholas of Tolentino for Città di Castello (1500-1501). Active chiefly in Urbino, but few works certainly his are known. On the basis of style, a small group of pictures is now ascribed to him, all connected with artistic activities centering on the Ducal Palace at Urbino.

One of the most interesting and versatile personalities of the later Quattrocento, equally successful as painter, sculptor and architect. But he did his most important work as an architect and theorist, working out a conception of space which anticipated that of the Cinquecento. Trained as a painter at Siena, he worked at first in an archaic style, not assimilating the innovations of Florentine painting until after 1470. At Urbino in 1477 as military engineer in the service of Federico di Montefeltro. Here he admired the work of Piero della Francesca and Luciano Laurana and wrote a treatise on civil and military engineering. Carved a remarkable *Scourging of Christ* in flattened relief *(stiacciato)* giving more scope for perspective effects. Worked at Gubbio and Iesi. His architectural masterpiece is the church of Santa Maria del Calcinaio near Cortona (1484-1486).

A particularly prolific painter in Bologna and the province of Emilia generally, active also as goldsmith, medallist and sculptor. Trained in Ferrara, he followed the lead of Perugino. His figures are graceful, though a little mincing and academic, despite a certain poetry. Raphael admired his Madonnas;

Michelangelo disliked him and called him a "dolt." A painter very popular in his day and for long afterwards. Among his most famous pictures are the *Marriage of St Cecilia* (Oratory of St Cecilia, Bologna), *Madonna in a Rose Garden* (Munich Pinakothek), and a *Pietà* (National Gallery, London).

GIOCONDO FRA (Verona c. 1433-Rome 1515) 94, 113.

His real name was Giovanni da Verona. He was an important figure in the architecture of Venetia, where he diffused the Renaissance style. Active chiefly in Verona (Loggia del Consiglio) and Venice, though also in South Italy and France. Translated Vitruvius' treatise on architecture and was called by the pope to collaborate with Raphael (1514) on the construction of the new St Peter's. A notable theorist and military engineer, he left many architectural designs.

GIOTTO (1266-1337) 14.

GIOVANNI DA UDINE (Udine 1487-Rome 1564) 94, 98, 121.

His real name was Giovanni di Francesco Ricamador. Trained in a provincial workshop at Udine near Venice, he came to Rome as one of Raphael's assistants, painting the musical instruments in the *St Cecilia* (Bologna). He specialized in painting the ornaments known as grotesques or arabesques (composed of medallions, foliage, scrolls, etc.) which, so popular in classical antiquity, were revived in Renaissance art. Raphael used him to paint such ornaments in the Vatican Loggie. He did other decorations in the Vatican and designed the borders of Raphael's tapestries. Cardinal de' Medici (later Pope Clement VII) employed him to decorate the Villa Madama in Rome with grotesques and small stucco panels. He also worked in the Farnesina, Rome, the Palazzo Vecchio, Florence, the Sala dei Pontefici in the Vatican (for

Clement VII), and the new sacristy of San Lorenzo, Florence. Returned to his native Udine in about 1539, there devoting himself chiefly to architecture and being placed in charge of public works in the town. Also worked in the Palazzo Grimani in Venice and decorated the palaces of Spilimbergo and Colloredo. Went back to Rome in 1560 to work on the second storey of the Vatican Loggie.

GIOVIO PAOLO (Como 1483-Florence 1552) 86.

Studied medicine at Padua and Pavia and became a prominent figure at the papal court, first of Leo X, then of Clement VII. He traveled widely and was loaded with honors. His villa at Como was adorned with frescoes designed by Giorgio Vasari; there he brought together a museum of rarities and curios. A voluminous writer, known for his history of his own time and his biographies of famous men, including Raphael.

GIULIO ROMANO (Rome 1499-Mantua 1546) 73, 94, 95, 104, 116, 121, 124.

Giulio Pippi, better known as Giulio Romano, was a pupil of Raphael. He very soon showed such talent that the master entrusted him with the execution of many parts of his work in the Stanze, the Loggie and certain altarpieces. Under Raphael he also started working as an architect in planning and building Villa Madama, Giulio de' Medici's country house on Monte Mario outside Rome. Baldassare Castiglione presented him to the Gonzagas of Mantua, where he did a great deal of work in the Ducal Palace, which he restored, enlarged, and decorated. For the same family he built the Palazzo del Te in Mantua, an edifice of refined proportions of which he decorated the interior with frescoes, and several other buildings. He invented a language of a certain originality synthesizing and combining Raphael's methods with the art of Michelangelo.

Gubbio (Umbria) 13; Ducal Palace 14.

INGRES Jean-Dominique (1780-1867) 7, 23, 126.

ISAAC Heinrich (c. 1445-1517) 89.

JOSQUIN DES PREZ (1450-1521) 89.

A composer who probably received his training at the Cambrai school of plain chant. He was influenced simultaneously by the musical environment of the court of Burgundy and that of Galeazzo Maria Sforza in Milan, where he lived with other French and Flemish artists from 1474 to 1479. In the latter year he went to Rome where he was employed by Cardinal Ascanio Sforza. He also worked at Ferrara, where he composed a mass for Duke Ercole d'Este. From 1486 to about 1495 he was precentor of the papal choir. Then he went back to France, acting as choirmaster in Paris and Cambrai. He composed masses, motets, psalms, chants characterized by an intense lyricism.

JULIUS II (Savona 1443-Rome 1513) 14, 50, 62, 67, 68, 73/75, 79, 85, 86, 89, 94, 95, 98, 113, 121.

One of the most important of the Renaissance popes, both as a statesman and a patron of the arts. Born Giuliano della Rovere, a member of an influential aristocratic family, he was made a cardinal by Sixtus IV and was elected pope in 1503. Embarked on a long series of military campaigns and diplomatic maneuvers in an attempt to restore the political power of the papal states. Attracted to his court the greatest writers and artists of his time. Commissioned Michelangelo to design his tomb and decorate the Sistine Chapel, Raphael to decorate the Vatican Stanze, Bramante to rebuild St Peter's. The work he set in motion all over Rome transformed the architectural aspect of the city.

JUSTUS OF GHENT (Ghent c. 1435-after 1480) 14, 17.

Very few documents have been preserved concerning this Flemish painter, who worked mainly in Italy. In 1464 he is mentioned as a member of the Guild of St Luke at Ghent and we know that he was at Urbino from 1473 to 1475. There is no record of him after 1480. Duke Federico di Montefeltro summoned him to Urbino to decorate his study, along with Pedro Berruguete. There he also painted the altarpiece of the *Communion of the Apostles* (Galleria Nazionale, Urbino). While some of his paintings reflect Italian influence, he in turn influenced several Italian painters, notably Giovanni Santi, Raphael's father.

LANDINO Cristoforo (Florence 1424-1492) 13, 17.

A famous humanist who lectured on poetry and rhetoric at Florence University, he was also a member of the Neo-Platonic Academy. His reputation rests on the *Disputationes Camaldulenses*, written about 1475 and published in 1480—a series of imaginary discussions which he supposed took place in the Camaldolite monastery in 1468 between Lorenzo de' Medici and Leon Battista Alberti and between the latter and Marsilio Ficino; others who took part were Giuliano de' Medici, Alamanno Rinuccini, Piero and Donato Acciaioli and Landino himself. The typically humanistic subject was the relationship between contemplative and active life, between culture and action. Landino played an important part in spreading humanist culture and classical literature. His commentaries on the Aeneid and the Divina Commedia are also worthy of notice. The manuscript of the latter work, illustrated by Botticelli, was presented to the Signoria (Government of the Florentine Republic) in 1481.

Laocoon (Pio Clementino Museum, Vatican) 84/86.

LAURANA Francesco (active c. 1453-1502) 24, 25, 27.

Sculptor of Dalmatian origin, of whose background little is known. The recorded dates of his career run from about 1453 to 1502, but there are considerable gaps. He is known to have worked in France (after 1458), in Naples, in Palermo (1468), at Urbino, and again in France. Clearly influenced by Antonello da Messina, Piero della Francesca, the Lombard masters, and Franco-Flemish art. Yet his style is highly original in its expressive synthesis tending toward a geometrization of forms particularly noticeable in the *Virgin and Child* (several versions) and the portraits (Eleonora and Beatrice of Aragon, Battista Sforza). His figures have an impressive spiritual calm and detachment, facial expression being reduced to an almost metaphysical minimum.

LAURANA Luciano (1420-Pesaro 1479) 13, 14, 27.

We know that Laurana, a Dalmatian by birth, was at Urbino about 1466, where he designed the Ducal Palace (1468) for Federico di Montefeltro. Little is known about his training, but he was very likely acquainted with Leon Battista Alberti's pioneer work, through his connection with the Gonzagas of Mantua, even before he went to Urbino. The Ducal Palace there is his masterpiece; it owes its novelty to the harmonious articulation of the various parts of the edifice centered around a quadrangle whose classical forms are at once severe and elegant, and to the varying treatment of the façades (of which one is attuned to the hill on which it rises, the other to the square it overlooks). Here he created the typical residence of a humanist prince, formal, elegant, dignified and severe—the reverse of ostentatious.

LEO X (1475-1521) 7, 14, 89, 98, 100, 101, 104, 105, 113, 115, 121, 128.

Giovanni de' Medici, son of Lorenzo the Magnificent, was educated by Poliziano and other humanists at his father's court in Florence. He was appointed Cardinal by Innocent VIII at the age of 13 and elected Pope on the death of Julius II in 1513. His period as Pope was fraught with difficulties and witnessed the first Lutheran schism. His nepotistic policy greatly benefited the Medici family. It can be counted to his credit that he patronized artists and men of letters and promoted culture. Bibbiena was his adviser and his secretaries included Pietro Bembo, Sadoleto and others. He patronized Baldassare Castiglione and Sannazzaro, besides employing Guiccardini, Giovio, Trissino and Ariosto. During his reign, Raphael and Michelangelo continued the works they had commenced under Julius II.

LEONARDO DA VINCI (Vinci 1452-Amboise 1519) 16, 17, 23, 34, 36, 40, 41, 46/50, 52, 58, 61, 79, 86, 95, 98, 104.

After being trained in the Florentine workshop of Verrocchio, Leonardo helped to renew and reorient late 15th-century art in Florence. His exceptional personality embodies the passionate quest for universal knowledge typical of the Renaissance and he took up painting as the best means to attain that goal. In his very first works he already sought to render the natural connection of human figure and surrounding space—from the *Annunciation* to the *Adoration of the Magi* (both in the Uffizi) and the *St Jerome* (in the Vatican Gallery), which mark a turning point in his study of light. In 1482 Leonardo left Florence for the court of Ludovico il Moro at Milan, where he worked as architect, military and hydraulic engineer, painter and sculptor, was surrounded by a large group of pupils. The *Virgin of the Rocks* and the *Last Supper* in Santa Maria delle Grazie (1495-1497) show what could be achieved as regards expression by the use of "sfumato" (shading), which Leonardo employed for a dynamic perspective where every detail is integrated in the changing, luminous atmosphere. His attention was diverted from painting by speculative interests, which resulted in a quantity of drawings, writings, notes and scientific experiments of various kinds. At the fall of Ludovico il Moro, he left Milan, traveling continually for a time. Returning to Florence he designed the cartoons for the *St Anne* and the *Battle of Anghiari* for Palazzo Vecchio. There too he painted the *Mona Lisa*. Leaving Florence, he returned to Milan and Lombardy. In 1513 he was in Rome, but finding the intellectual milieu uncongenial he accepted Francis I's invitation and emigrated to France, dying at the Château d'Amboise.

We know very little about Lotto's training; even the place and date of his birth are uncertain. But there is no doubt that his sensibility and culture were typically Venetian, based on Bellini and showing points of contact with various artists, from the Vivarinis to Giorgione and Palma, and even Albrecht Dürer. He travelled a great deal and worked at Treviso, various cities on the Venetian mainland, in the Marche and in Rome, where he was summoned by Julius II to decorate the Stanze and remained until about 1512. From there he went to Bergamo until 1525, then again to Venice and Treviso, finally to Loreto, where he died. He was particularly open to tonal problems and the great importance of the landscape. During his mature period he moved steadily toward a stricter design and purer colors, showing great variety and originality in his choice of subjects. His close links with Rome and the great masters of the Tuscan tradition did not alter a vision that was basically Venetian.

His real name was Tommaso Cassaio; Masaccio is a nickname meaning, roughly, "Big Tom." His life is not well documented. Entered the guild of physicians and apothecaries in Florence in 1422, the painters' guild (confraternity of St Luke) in 1424. According to Vasari he then began collaborating with Masolino (meaning "Little Tom"). They worked together on the altarpiece with the *Virgin and Child with St Anne*, the decorations in the chapel of St Catherine in San Clemente, Rome, and the Brancacci Chapel frescoes in the Carmine church in Florence. From Masaccio were ordered in 1426 the *Trinity* fresco in Santa Maria Novella, Florence, and a polyptych for the Carmine church in Pisa (now dismembered: central panel with *Virgin and Child* in London, upper tier with *Crucifixion* in Naples, side panels in Pisa). After Masolino's departure for Hungary in 1427, he continued the Brancacci Chapel frescoes alone with the story of St Peter *(St Peter Baptizing, St Peter and St John Distributing Alms, St Peter Healing the Sick, The Tribute Money)* and *Adam and Eve Cast Out of Paradise*. The Brancacci Chapel is Masaccio's masterpiece: these frescoes, in their concern with man and the human condition as distinct from the divine, in their sober realism, their solidity of form and their masterly spatial effects, mark the first radical innovation in early 15th-century painting.

One of the key figures of Renaissance art, owing to his achievements as sculptor, painter, architect, poet. Trained in Ghirlandaio's workshop in Florence, then in the school set up in the Medici Gardens under the sculptor Bertoldo. His early contacts with the humanists at the court of Lorenzo the Magnificent initiated him into that Neo-Platonic culture which shaped his whole conception of art. Instinctively drawn to sculpture, but practiced painting and architecture with equal brilliance. His long life spanned momentous developments in Renaissance art, a period of restless search and experiment vividly reflected in his dramatic conception of humanity. After his youthful activity in Florence and Bologna, he made his first stay in Rome in 1498-1499 (*Pietà* in St Peter's). Then he carved the gigantic *David* in Florence (1501) and began his activity as a painter. In 1504 he painted the *Doni Tondo* (Uffizi). That same year the Florentine Republic ordered the fresco of the *Battle of Cascina*: it was never executed and only the preliminary sketches remain. In 1505 Julius II asked him to make his tomb, a vast monument with many figures; it was never completed, but work on it, and troubles connected with it, dragged on for the rest of Michelangelo's life and he gloomily referred to it as "the Tragedy of the Tomb." Meanwhile for Julius II he painted the ceiling of the Sistine Chapel (1508-1512), for Leo X he designed the façade of San Lorenzo in Florence (1516-1520, never executed), and for Giulio de' Medici the Medici Chapel in San Lorenzo and the Laurentian Library in Florence. In 1536 he settled for good in Rome, painting the *Last Judgment* on the back wall of the Sistine Chapel (finished 1541) and frescoing the Cappella Paolina in the Vatican (1542-1550). From 1547 he supervised the construction of St Peter's, returning to the central plan of Bramante: he only had time to build the apse. Designed or redesigned several buildings in Rome and, in his last years, carved the three great Pietàs (Florence Cathedral, Castello Sforzesco, Milan, and Palestrina Pietà).

Milan 16, 27, 105;
Ambrosiana 75, 77/79; Brera 34, 35; Santa Maria presso San Satiro 22, 27.

MONTEFELTRO Federico di (1422-1482) 13/15, 17, 18, 23, 25.

A natural son of Guidantonio, Count of Montefeltro and Urbino, he became lord of Urbino after the murder of his half brother Oddantonio (1444). Educated at Mantua under Vittorino da Feltre, one of the most famous teachers of the Renaissance, and schooled in arms in Lombardy under Niccolo Piccinino, he became one of the most remarkable rulers of the Renaissance, a scholar and humanist, a patron of the arts, and an able general and statesman. Playing off one power against another as he sought to consolidate and extend his dominions, he allied himself with the Sforzas of Milan, with the Aragonese kings of Naples, with the pope against the Malatestas of Rimini, and then with the latter against the pope. Ably seconded by his wife Battista Sforza, he made Urbino one of the leading artistic and intellectual centers of the Renaissance, gathering around him a cultivated circle of artists, writers and philosophers. Luciano Laurana designed the Ducal Palace, while Berruguete, Justus of Ghent, Melozzo da Forlì, Baccio Pontelli, Francesco di Giorgio Martini and others decorated it. Bramante got his start in Urbino. Federico was the friend and patron of Piero della Francesca, who painted portraits of the duke and his wife (Uffizi, Florence).

MONTEFELTRO Guidobaldo di (1472-1508) 13, 14, 17, 23, 27.

Son of Federico di Montefeltro and Battista Sforza. Educated in the humanist environment of Urbino. A capable general, he fought against the French in Romagna and Campania. In 1502 Cesare Borgia's ambiguous policy cost him his duchy, which he won back and lost again, only regaining final possession after Pope Alexander VI's death in 1503. He offered hospitality at Urbino to Pope Julius II when the latter travelled to Bologna. His wife Elisabetta Gonzaga failed to give him a son, so Guidobaldo adopted his nephew Francesco Maria della Rovere. His name is linked with the splendid patronage of his court, which continued the tradition initiated by his father and was portrayed in Baldassare Castiglione's "Book of the Courtier."

Naples, Museo di Capodimonte 16.
Narbonne, Cathedral 128.

NAVAGERO Andrea (Venice 1483-Blois 1529) 113.

Also called Naugerius. Poet, orator, statesman, collaborator of Aldus Manutius the Elder, and a notable scholar. Composed funeral orations for the Venetian Republic and was librarian to Cardinal Bessarion, who had brought together an unrivaled collection of Greek manuscripts. Served as Venetian ambassador in Spain and appointed official historian of the Republic with the task of completing Sabellico's unfinished *History of Venice*, but died before he could do so. He wrote a learned commentary on Aristotle's *Poetics*.

Neo-Platonic ideal 13, 79, 89, 98, 121.

Oxford, Ashmolean Museum 25, 43, 46, 48, 110, 111.

PACE Luigi 115.
PACIOLI Luca (1445-c. 1510) 14, 16.

PALLADIO Andrea (Padua 1508-Venice 1580) 114, 115, 121.

Early taken up by Count Giangiorgio Trissino whose intelligent patronage oriented him toward architecture and gave him a solid classical culture. Taken to Rome by Trissino where he studied and drew the ancient monuments, from which he derived the principles of his own style of design. After the Villa Godi at Lonedo, he designed the Basilica Palladiana (1549), the Chiericati Palace and other buildings in Vicenza, followed by a series of villas admirably adapted to their landscape setting (La Malcontenta, Villa Capra, Villa Barbaro at Maser, etc.). He wrote an influential treatise on architecture. The many buildings he erected in Vicenza changed the face of the city. Toward the end of his life he worked in Venice, designing two of its finest Renaissance churches, San Giorgio Maggiore and the Redentore. His last great work was the Teatro Olimpico in Vicenza, the final expression of his vision of space in which light plays a determinant part.

PANOFSKY Erwin 34.
Paris, Louvre 26, 27, 34, 37, 40, 52; Cabinet des Dessins 22, 118, 119.

PARMIGIANINO (Parma 1503-1540) 114, 115, 121.

His real name was Francesco Maria Mazzola. Trained in the workshop of his two uncles Michele and Ilario Mazzola, modest provincial painters, he came into contact with Correggio after the latter's arrival in Parma in 1518. The grace of Correggio's style appears in his earliest works, his frescoes in San Giovanni Evangelista in Parma, but with an original accent of his own, an elongation and suppleness in the figures which became more and more marked as he grew older. In Rome in 1523, where he saw the work of Michelangelo and Raphael, which he assimilated into his own aristocratic ideal of beauty

(*St Jerome*, National Gallery, London). Met Polidoro da Caravaggio. After the Sack of Rome (1527) he went to Bologna where he painted several altarpieces which mark the beginnings of Mannerism. Commissioned to paint frescoes in Santa Maria della Steccata in Parma in 1530, but he neglected his work in favor of alchemy and got into trouble with the ecclesiastics, who finally ordered his arrest for breach of contract. Also did some frescoes in the castle of Fontanellato near Parma (story of Diana and Actaeon). Ill, and increasingly eccentric and neurotic, he retired to Casalmaggiore near Cremona, where he spent the last year or two of his life.

Pasti Matteo de' 20.
Paul III Farnese, Pope (1534-1549) 68.
Pellegrino da Modena (1460/65-1523) 121.

Penni Giovanni Francesco (Florence c. 1488-Naples 1528) 94, 104, 121, 124.

Worked as Raphael's assistant in the later Roman works (Loggie, Farnesina, tapestries, Stanza dell'Incendio). After Raphael's death, he continued, with Giulio Romano, the decoration of the Sala di Costantino in the Vatican (1524-1525), where he appears to have painted the monochromes on the plinth, the *Baptism of Constantine* and the *Donation of Rome*. He may have had some share in other works by Raphael. He was also a prolific painter of easel pictures, chiefly on religious themes.

Perino del Vaga (c. 1500-1547) 68, 94, 121.

Little is known of where Pietro Bonaccorsi (such was his real name) got his training; it may have been in the Florentine workshop of Ridolfo del Ghirlandaio or Fra Bartolomeo. He got his nickname from a painter called Il Vaga who took him to Rome, where he studied the works of Raphael and Michelangelo and made some drawings of ancient monuments. There he met

Giovanni Francesco Penni and Giulio Romano, through whom he found work in the Vatican Loggie. In the Vatican he also decorated, together with Giovanni da Udine, the Sala dei Pontefici in the Borgia apartments. He worked, too, in several Roman churches. Forced to leave Rome after the sack of the city (1527), he went to Genoa where he decorated the Doria Palace besides working for many churches and noble families. After a spell at Pisa, working in the Cathedral, he returned to Genoa and was elected head of the painters' guild. He finally settled in Rome, where he was highly considered and received a great many commissions. One of the most able followers of Raphael, from whom he is distinguished by a decorative naturalism that is the antithesis of the classical ideal.

Perugia 23, 28, 33, 40, 41, 50, 61, 62, 79;
Cathedral 40;
San Francesco al Prato (Baglioni chapel) 58, 61;
Collegio del Cambio 33, 34, 40.

Perugino (Città della Pieve c. 1445-1523) 23, 28, 33, 34, 36, 40, 41, 50, 58, 67, 73, 90, 98, 104, 124.

Pietro Vannucci, after spending many years in Perugia from which he got his nickname, went to Florence where he was in Verrocchio's workshop in 1472. Most of his work was done in Florence, Rome, Perugia and several towns in the Marche, besides Bologna, Cremona, Pavia and Venice. He was a member of the group of Tuscan painters (Botticelli, Cosimo Rosselli and Ghirlandaio) commissioned to decorate the Sistine Chapel. The layout of his fresco of *Christ Delivering the Keys to St Peter* later influenced Raphael's *Marriage of the Virgin*. Between 1498 and 1500 he finished the decoration of the Collegio del Cambio in Perugia. Though he was closely linked with Tuscan art and felt the influence of Piero della Francesca, his work shows a delicate lyrical quality

and a sensitive feeling for the atmosphere of a landscape that is typically Umbrian.

Peruzzi Baldassare (Siena 1481-Rome 1536) 67, 73, 90, 94, 116, 122/124.

A Sienese in culture and sensibility, Peruzzi worked chiefly in Rome and Siena both as painter and architect. He attained a position of the first importance owing to the originality with which he set his buildings in their surroundings. His architectural works comprise the Farnesina Palace built for Agostino Chigi after 1505 (the interior of which he decorated with paintings, the most original being the *trompe-l'œil* frescoes of the Sala delle Prospettive); Palazzo Massimo, whose curved façade was an entirely new departure, and several other buildings. He also worked as an architect at Carpi (near Modena) and Bologna. As a painter, too, he was very prolific (frescoes in Santa Maria della Pace, Sant'Onofrio and San Pietro in Montorio, Rome).

Petrarch (1304-1374) 86.
Piccolomini Aeneas Sylvius (Pope Pius II, 1458-1464) 41;
Francesco Todeschini (Pope Pius III, 1503) 41.

Piero della Francesca (Borgo San Sepolcro c. 1420-1492) 14/16, 23, 27, 36, 40, 41, 58, 67, 104, 124.

We know that Piero while still very young worked under Domenico Veneziano on the Sant'Egidio frescoes in Florence, but we know very little about his previous training. After Florence, where he may have learnt from his master the use of bright, atmospheric light, he returned to Borgo San Sepolcro (where in 1445 he was commissioned to paint the *Madonna of Mercy* polyptych, which he did not finish until about 1462). Then he went to Ferrara, Rimini (1451) and Arezzo, where he produced his masterpiece: the Story of the True Cross in the choir of San Francesco (1452-1466). He interrupted his work at

Arezzo by trips to Rome, Borgo San Sepolcro and Urbino where in 1469 he stayed with Giovanni Santi, Raphael's father. For many years Duke Federico di Montefeltro was his friend and patron. Piero was an influential personality at the court of Urbino. There too, as well as in Florence, he had an opportunity to come in touch with Flemish art currents. His aim was to achieve a synthesis of the volumes that should concentrate the beholder's interest on the figures, while at the time using light in a very peculiar manner (Senigallia *Virgin*; *Virgin and Saints*, Brera). He wrote a treatise *De prospectiva pingendi* and a study *De quinque corporibus regolaribus*; the latter was dedicated to Guidobaldo di Montefeltro after 1482.

PINTURICCHIO (Perugia c. 1454-Siena 1513) 41.

Bernardino di Betto, better known as Pinturicchio, belonged to the Umbrian school of Perugino. Among his early paintings are the *Scenes from the Life of San Bernardino* now in the Perugia museum, which already show the characteristic airiness of his spatial composition and the virtuoso treatment of fabulous subjects that he maintained his whole life long. He did a great deal of work in Rome and in Umbria, collaborating with Perugino in the Sistine Chapel, decorating the mansions and private chapels of the Roman nobility, and fulfilling many commissions in the Vatican. Among his most important works are the decoration of the Bufalini Chapel in Santa Maria in Aracoeli, the Borgia apartments in the Vatican (commissioned by Pope Alexander VI in 1493-1494), the Eroli Chapel in Spoleto Cathedral, and the Baglioni Chapel at Spello. After 1502 he lived almost entirely at Siena, where he did various frescoes in the Cathedral, chief among them the decoration of the Piccolomini Library.

PLATO (429-347 B.C.) 17, 86, 89.
PLINY the Elder (23-79 A.D.) 85.

POLIDORO DA CARAVAGGIO (Bergamo c. 1500-1546) 121.

Polidoro Caldara—to give him his real name—went to Rome at a very early age and worked under Giovanni da Udine in the Vatican Loggie. As a follower of Raphael, he did a great deal of work in collaboration with Maturino, making his mark with frescoes in grisaille decorating the façades of private mansions and their interiors. Unfortunately very little of this work has been preserved, though a number of prints are still extant. He also did some frescoes of decorative landscapes in San Silvestro al Quirinale. Subsequently he worked at Naples and in Sicily. He initiated a peculiar taste that transmuted Raphael's classical forms into elegant decorations characterized by refinements of drawing and chiaroscuro.

POLLAIOLO Antonio Benci del (Florence 1431/32-Rome 1498) 44, 58.

Goldsmith, draftsman, painter, sculptor and engraver, Pollaiolo was one of the most representative and original Italian artists of the 15th century. Vasari says that he was a pupil of Lorenzo Ghiberti; but in fact he probably got his first training as a goldsmith in the workshop of Vittorio Ghiberti. In 1457 he received the first commission of which we have certain knowledge— the reliquary for San Giovanni in Florence, executed in collaboration with Milano Dei and Betto Betti (now in the Museum of the Opera del Duomo). In the following years he did a great many works in metal and after 1466 designed embroidered vestments for San Giovanni. In 1467 or 1468 he was appointed with Verrocchio, Luca della Robbia and other artists to a committee set up for the purpose of placing the globe on top of the lantern that crowns the cupola of Santa Maria del Fiore. He also executed a number of paintings either alone or in collaboration with his brother Piero. In 1484 he was summoned to Rome and started work on the bronze

tomb of Pope Sixtus IV in the Vatican Grottoes, which he finished in 1493. In 1497 he executed the tomb of Innocent VIII in St Peter's.

POLYDOROS of Rhodes (2nd century B.C.) 85.

PONZIO Flaminio (c. 1560-1613) 90.

RAIMONDI Marcantonio (c. 1480-before 1534) 95.

RAPHAEL (1483-1520), works mentioned: for Città di Castello: *Processional banner*, for the Confraternity of Charity (1499), Pinacoteca communale 23;
altarpiece of the Blessed Nicholas of Tolentino (1501) 33;
paintings:
Entombment of Christ (1507) 56/59, 61; *Esterhazy Madonna* (1505-1507) 53, 61; *Foligno Madonna* (1511-1512) 104; *Granduca Madonna* (1504-1505) 50, 51, 61; *The Knight's Dream* (1504-1505) 34, 38, 50, 58, 104; *Madonna of the Goldfinch* (c. 1507) 53, 54, 61; *Madonna of the Meadow* (1506) 31, 41, 53, 55, 61; *Marriage of the Virgin* (1504) 34, 35, 40, 41, 58, 90, 104; *Prophet Isaiah* (1511-1512) 102; *Sistine Madonna* (1513-1514) 126; *St Cecilia* (1514) 98, 99, 126; *St Michael and the Dragon* (1504-1505) 34, 37, 50, 58; *Three Graces* (1504-1505) 34, 39, 50, 58, 104; *Transfiguration* (1518-1520) 128, 129; *Vision of Ezekiel* (after 1516) 112, 113, 126; portraits: *Baldassare Castiglione* (1514-1515) 26, 27, 104; *Portrait of a Cardinal* (1510-1511) 101, 104; *Portrait of a Lady with a Veil ("Donna Velata")* (c. 1516) 102/104, 124; with Giulio Romano: *La Fornarina* (c. 1518-1519) 124, 125; *Julius II* (1512) 74; *Pope Leo X with Cardinals Giulio de' Medici and Luigi de' Rossi* (c. 1518) 100, 101, 104; *Maddalena Doni* (c. 1506) 61;
– Stanze of the Vatican:
Stanza di Eliodoro (1511-1514) 27, 68, 69, 72, 73, 88, 90/95, 98, 102, 104, 121;

Little is known of Raphael's father for only his later life is documented. We know that he had a workshop as painter and decorator in Urbino, that he worked for the Montefeltro family, by whom he was greatly esteemed, and at the court of Mantua. He was also a town councillor and married Magia, daughter of Battista Ciarla. He worked chiefly in the Marche, where several of his altarpieces are extant. Though he responded to the cultivated environment of Urbino, and to the teaching of Melozzo da Forlì and Piero della Francesca, he never succeeded in finding a truly original style and remained prisoner of an eclecticism which, however polished and refined, was characterized by a chilly virtuosity. Giovanni Santi wrote a rhymed Chronicle of the life of Federico di Montefeltro that gives a tolerably good idea of his aesthetic principles.

Sebastiano Luciani, better known as Sebastiano del Piombo, received his artistic training in Venice under the influence of Giovanni Bellini. We know that he worked with Giorgione, from whom he differs by an architectural, classicistic feeling for form and composition. In Rome, where he went in 1511, he found a cultural environment that was naturally congenial. The direct experience of Michelangelo, whom he took as his ideal model, led him to study the problems of movement and sculptural form. Raphael, to whom he felt less strongly attracted, incited him to concentrate on drawing and majestic proportions. In Rome he painted the Sala dei Pianeti in the Farnesina Palace for Agostino Chigi and a *Scourging of Christ* for San Pietro in Montorio (1517-1524). This latter work proves how well he assimilated his masters' teaching and marks a first step on the road to Mannerism. Sebastiano del Piombo was also a portrait painter of considerable ability.

Though probably an assistant of Piero della Francesca at Arezzo, Signorelli was closely connected with Pollaiolo and the Florentine school from which he derived a strong feeling for line and for sculptural form as well as for luminous space. He worked with Bartolomeo della Gatta on a fresco in the Sistine Chapel *(Testament and Death of Moses)*. For Tuscan and Umbrian churches he produced many works (*Scourging of Christ*, Brera, Milan; *Circumcision*, London; *Education of Pan*, Berlin; altarpiece in Perugia Cathedral, etc.). From 1492 to 1502 he decorated the Chapel of San Brizio in Orvieto Cathedral with frescoes in which he achieves dramatic effects with vigorous sculptural forms (*Last Judgment* and *Antichrist*).

Giovanni Antonio Bazzi, better known as Sodoma, received his training in the workshop of Martino Spanzotti, a painter of the Piedmontese school. He was greatly influenced by the works of Leonardo which he saw in Milan. In 1501 he went to Siena and worked on several fresco cycles in Tuscany, notably at Monte Oliveto Maggiore and San Gimignano. He went to Rome in 1508 to work in the Stanza della Segnatura and returned there in 1514 to work for Agostino Chigi in the Farnesina Palace *(Marriage of Alexander and Roxana)*. He travelled a great deal in Tuscany and elsewhere, but did most of his work at Siena. Though he misunderstood both Leonardo and Raphael, theirs is the most marked influence revealed in the works of Sodoma's mature period, where the emotive tone of his elegant forms is stressed by a vaporous chiaroscuro.

After receiving a thorough artistic and cultural training at Arezzo, Vasari spent three years in Florence in the workshops of Andrea del Sarto and Baccio Bandinelli. This was followed by a long period of travels and a variety of commissions. In 1531 he was summoned to Rome by Cardinal Ippolito de' Medici. From there he returned to Arezzo and Florence, where he was entrusted with the decoration of the town for the visit of the Emperor Charles V in 1533. After further travels (including a stay with Pietro Aretino in Venice in 1541) he went back to Rome as a protégé of Alessandro Farnese. This gave him an opportunity to associate with Michelangelo who had always been his highest ideal and advised him to devote himself chiefly to architecture, an art that he found particularly congenial. In fact he did a great deal of work for Paul III and Julius III in and around Rome. He designed the Uffizi (the offices of the judiciary) in Florence and the Palace and Church of the Knights at Pisa in 1561. From Pius V he received a commission for the frescoes in the Sala Regia and three chapels in the Vatican. At the same time, acting on the advice of Paolo Giovio, Alessandro Farnese and even Michelangelo himself, Vasari was writing his *Vite de' più eccellenti pittori, scultori et architettori* (Lives of the Most Excellent Painters, Sculptors and Architects). The first edition, up to Michelangelo, was published in 1550 and a second, enlarged edition in 1568. Although the information it contains is not always very reliable, it is a work of the utmost importance.

A cultivated collector of ancient manuscripts, which he supplied to the libraries of the great humanist princes—the Estes of Ferrara, the Medici of Florence, the Aragonese of Naples, Matthias Corvinus of Hungary, and Federico di Montefeltro of Urbino. From 1440 to 1480 his bookshop in Florence was the meeting place of the leading men of letters of the age. When printing became widespread he retired from trade and wrote the *Vite* (Lives) of the many people he had known. Besides being a source of interesting information, the work is an example of lively vernacular prose.

Vincenzo Tamagni, as he was christened, was a mediocre painter who copied Sodoma and felt the influence of many different artists. But he was first and foremost an imitator of Raphael and may have worked in the Stanze. In any case, he did a great deal of work in Rome but it is no easy matter to discover exactly which paintings are his.

PUBLISHED SEPTEMBER 1967

TEXT AND ILLUSTRATIONS PRINTED IN OFFSET
BY IMPRIMERIES RÉUNIES S.A., LAUSANNE

PHOTOGRAPHS BY

Alinari, Florence (pages 16, 17, 21, 53, 77, 78, 97, 126), Maurice Babey, Basel (12, 18, 24, 26, 37, 54, 64-65, 69, 70, 71, 72, 76, 80, 81, 82, 83, 87, 88, 91, 92, 96, 106, 107, 108, 112, 116, 122, 127, 129), Bertoni, Florence (page 42), Cameraphoto, Venice (page 47), Fotomero, Urbino (pages 10-11), John R. Freeman & Co., Ltd, London (page 38), Gabinetto Fotografico Nazionale, Rome (page 114), Giraudon, Paris (pages 39, 51, 60, 103), Charlandré Jobin, Geneva (page 120), Erwin Meyer, Vienna (pages 30-31, 55), La Photothèque, Paris (pages 19, 34), Publifoto, Milan (title page), Rampazzi Ferruccio, Turin (page 20), Scala, Florence (pages 15, 35, 59, 99, 100, 101, 117, 125), Geo Spearman, Windsor (pages 45, 85, 119), Toso Mirco, Mestre, Venice (page 27), and by courtesy of the following museums and collections: Berlin, Staatliche Museen (page 19), Chatsworth, Devonshire Collections (page 74), Florence, Uffizi (pages 93, 114), London, British Museum (pages 44, 49, 56, 57), London, National Gallery (page 52), Oxford, Ashmolean Museum (pages 25, 43, 46, 48, 110, 111), Vatican City, Vatican Library and Pontifical Museums (pages 84, 109), Versailles, Photographic Service of the French National Museums (pages 22, 118), and Fratelli Fabbri Editori, Milan (page 95).

Printed in Switzerland